TWO FEET FORWARD

Everyday Lessons in Leadership

Always, Two Feet In –

Heather Macy

Coach Heather Macy

TWO
FEET
FORWARD

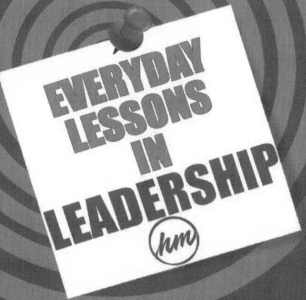

EVERYDAY
LESSONS
IN
LEADERSHIP

hm

HEATHER MACY

Forewords by Dr. Izzy Justice, Jeff Compher & Coach Sylvia Hatchell

ISBN: 0-9992125-4-0
ISBN-13: 978-0-9992125-4-7

MH
BookServices

Bulk or Team Sales are available by contacting
HeatherMacy@influenceandimpacters.com

**Proceeds from the book benefit the non-profit Influence and
Impacters, Inc. Learn more about this organization by visiting
influenceandimpacters.com**

Edited by Dr. Pamela Hopkins & Shannon Macy Swaim

Book Illustrations by Monica Mann

Book Produced by Jamy Bechler

Cover Design by Nicole Mealing

This book is dedicated to my parents, Claude and Jean; my sister, Shannon; and my niece and nephew, Hope and Seth: I love you all very much.

To Toni: Thank you! You will always be the best.

.

To Pamela: Thank you for always being the biggest cheerleader and support warrior.

To Nicole & Monica: Thank you for playing such big roles within this book. Both of you are great role models for athletes with multiple talents and gifts.

TABLE OF CONTENTS

FOREWORDS

L ife is always the best "lab" work. It is in life's challenges, ups and downs as we say, that learning can occur. That learning can be so powerful that it can change not only one's own life but also the lives of others by sharing those experiences. It's why we watch movies, read books, listen to speakers, and love mentors/coaches. Within life, I have always held that sports present a powerful microcosm of life itself. In one game, there can be many such ups and downs, many victories and failures, many disappointments and happy moments, many interactions within a team, many interactions with an opponent, and strategies by your coach and another coach trying to beat you down. Basketball is clearly such a sport and those who coach it and play it have many experiences to share. It's why we love sports and our sports heroes.

In this book, Coach Heather Macy shares many of the key experiences of her journey knowing that in her stories, both in her triumphs and defeats, in her genius and vulnerability, you can learn the same lessons she has learned. Her goal is simple: help others grow and become the best versions of themselves. I have seen Coach Macy evolve before my very eyes and am proud of the great work she has done to learn from her life and to transfer that knowledge to her athletes and her circle of influence. She has learned the most powerful of all lessons: the ultimate currency of life is happiness. Happy athletes perform better and happy people enjoy life more, both making their condition contagious. Armed with this truth, she shares in her first book powerful stories to help you grow wherever you are on your journey so that you may get to your happiness faster.

Using stories from personal and professional experiences, Coach Macy invites you to join her journey. It is almost impossible to not find yourself nodding and laughing and crying and learning all the way. I applaud what she has done in this book and highly recommend it.

DR. IZZY JUSTICE
Sports Neuropsychologist
Accomplished Author of 7 Books

I've worked in College Athletics for over 30 years. Along the way, I have met some wonderfully gifted student-athletes and had the opportunity to work with some extremely talented coaches. Every now and then you meet someone who is truly unique. Most would agree that the very best coaches are great motivators, and a few are able to go beyond that skill and become inspirational. Heather Macy is one of these coaches.

Heather is an optimist who believes that everyone is capable of living up to high standards to accomplish their goals. That trusting attitude is refreshing and uplifting, but it can also lead to disappointment, at least for some ... but not for Heather. She has managed to keep her positive outlook on life front and center, even in the face of adversity.

This book chronicles the lessons she has learned throughout her life and career as a player, assistant coach, and head coach in women's basketball. But don't be misled: this is not a "basketball book." This is a book about life that uses basketball as the backdrop for relatable stories that will touch everyone. She keeps you engaged with her refreshing style of honesty and humor.

Heather Macy is a head coach who is still coachable. When she said she was writing this book it did not come as a surprise to me. She was always reading from a stack of books on her desk about leadership and team building. She is a life-long learner who wants to share her knowledge and experiences with others. This played out in real life when she was asked to teach a course and she wanted to do it. After a lengthy discussion, we agreed it was something she should pursue.

So, if you can't sign up for her class, you should at least read her book. You will soon find out it is more than you expected...

> – *More about life than games;*
> – *More about relationships than coaching;*
> – *More about realizing long-term success than winning a single game.*

JEFF COMPHER
Former ECU Athletics Director
2012-13 Under Armour Athletics Director of the Year

I remember the day my friends and colleagues at Francis Marion University called and told me that they had hired a new *(small in status, but big and fiery in heart)* women's basketball coach. Wow! Now that was definitely an understatement! I had heard her name before but did not know much about her. As time passed, I learned a lot about this little passionate fireball coach and because my first 11 years as a college basketball coach was at Francis Marion University (*College when I was there*), we developed and grew a special relationship because of our great love for two things: Francis Marion University; and the game we both loved, basketball!

Just like Heather, this book speaks from her heart and shares how she has lived it. Every chapter is amazing and filled with valuable life lessons! As you read each chapter your mind is saying, Yes, I agree. She is exactly right. How does she know this? What a great lesson. It sounds like she knows me or knows exactly what I need to hear!

One of the things I admire about Heather is something I preach to my team each and every day! Heather is an assertive aggressive female! She has a tremendous work ethic and is passionate about what she believes! Heather is a winner and shares with us in this book what she believes and how she gets it done!

Thank you, Heather, for being an assertive aggressive female and for being bold and sharing with us your life stories about how you get it done! Keep it going, girl! My challenge to you and to everyone who reads this book: "Be the kind of woman that when her feet hit the floor in the morning the devil says, "Oh crap she's up!" That's just like Heather Macy. *You Go Girl!*

SYLVIA HATCHELL
UNC Tarheel Head Women's Basketball Coach
Winningest Coach in ACC History
1,000 Overall Wins

PREFACE

A NOTE TO THE READER ABOUT THIS "PLANE RIDE READ"

This book provides you with a pep talk and a short story within each chapter. It is meant to inspire and prepare you for and during life's challenges. The goal of this book is to enable you to finish this fun, simple, and short read on your next plane ride or beach trip. My hope is that you can take the ideas and inspiration with you throughout each day. It was written with love and with the intent to inspire you to live a full and happy life of influence and impact.

~ Heather Macy

- CHAPTER 1 -
GET A STOP

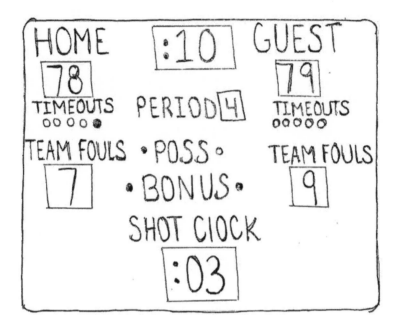

G et a stop, the crowd yells. I giggle to myself. "Get a stop, huh?" Well, the stop that was needed was four possessions ago in this game. The ability to recognize what is needed or required prior to everyone else in the room is a gift of experience and perspective. I do believe that most elite performers have a unique ability to recognize and act quickly. An amateur and a novice are only initially able to see the most obvious of decisions.

A good example in athletics is the average fan in the stands. Typically, a fan only sees it through one lens which is the immediate one that impacts their favorite team or player. As coaches gain experience and study the game, they also gain a unique perspective on winning and

> *The ability to recognize what is needed or required prior to everyone else in the room is a gift of experience and perspective.*

the actual flow of the game. I call this ability a G.A.S. Mindset (Get A Stop). The true beauty of it all happens when a person is able to do this daily in life. It's the ability to recognize in all situations when encouragement, a big hug, or even a tough decision may be needed. That is the key and timing is everything. It's definitely an ability that can be learned. I believe it is one that you can recognize the need for while practicing mindfulness each day. This is a learned skill and acting quickly will take tremendous courage.

When I improved at in-game coaching, I got better at recognizing when we needed the stop. In life, I also got better at recognizing when I needed to get a stop. Most of the time, I found that I was only reacting after a decision was made or it was to the point of no return. Examples would be things like a player coming in to request a transfer or a personal relationship ending. How did I not see it coming? I think for me, life was just moving so fast. Somedays, I had a hard time keeping my head above water. I would find myself attempting to check as many things as possible off of the to-do list and move on. I did not pay close enough attention to the moods, emotions, or habits of others. This would prove to be a costly mistake.

Sometimes, the right decision was right in front of my face. I recognized that I needed to develop the skill of anticipation. I needed to see it coming in advance, and I needed to learn that skill quickly. So, I started a process of reflection after each day. I would go back through each step, conversation, and activity of my day. It was kind of like watching film of a game. I began to pay close attention to what happened throughout that day. At night, I would immediately retrace the steps of the day to see what I may have possibly missed. If I believed that I may have missed something essential, I made a point to circle back with that person immediately. Now this was outside of my comfort zone, but it's a healthy exercise and it builds character. I narrowed in on other's emotions and especially on the advice or direction I had given. This technique worked and was very valuable. I was able to challenge myself in the same way that I would at a sporting event to get ahead of the possession and anticipate to be better prepared.

Maybe the most valuable skill in developing this ability for me was to acknowledge when I made an error. Sometimes the error was my response. Sometimes it was my patience. And other times, it had nothing to do with me. I became very aware of my listening skills. I learned to listen to the hurt, concern, and worry of others. I was listening to more than the actual words, and I listened to what was behind the words.

I do believe that I have been able to help prevent larger issues by becoming better and better at this G.A.S. mindset strategy. It has helped me learn from my mistakes and correct them right away. Making the same mistakes over and over again can become the toughest lessons to learn. I also think that it has created a lot more wins for everyone in my life. I always remind myself of the biblical phrase that reads, "For *such a time as this*." When something tough or unexpected happens, I am always reminded, *"For such a time as this."* Learn it, learn it quickly, and be prepared to recognize the next situation that will require a "Get A Stop" mindset.

MACYOLOGY:
FOR SUCH A TIME AS THIS

The Story

I lived in the little Village of Misenheimer. I arrived there with the opportunity to be a first-time head coach. I had great support and encouragement around me. It was what I had always wanted. My dream of running my own program had finally come true. It was a challenging opportunity, but one I was thrilled to accept.

During the first year, we were challenged in many different areas. The budget, the facility, the team, and sometimes even my inexperienced youth were challenges for us. One of the first things that I hung up in the basketball office was a sign that said, "For such a time as this." My college roommate had given me the sign as a reminder of the challenges we may face as we are preparing for something big. It became a daily reminder when new things flew my way. I gained more strength with each and every hurdle we crossed for the long race that was ahead. There were strange and weird days during my first opportunity at running a program. For me, that sign that hung above the doorway became a beacon of encouragement. Let's put it this way: I am thankful now that the newspaper in town only ran on Tuesdays and Thursdays. Actually, I'm not sure social media even existed. My mistakes were not broadcasted as they occurred as they would be today.

That was a season of firsts. I am embarrassed to say that I called a timeout that I did not have and lost a game. I assembled a team before I knew exactly how to build a team the right way. I even formulated an offensive and defensive system before I knew the personnel did not fit it. So basically, I was terrible. My life was very reactionary, and I hated it. This is when I first started to realize and explore different ways to approach a day and my life. I recognized very quickly that if I was going to continue to make mistakes and only learn this way, then it would be a long coaching career ahead or a short one depending upon how you see it.

I'm not sure why I was afforded the incredible opportunity to become a head coach at 26 years old, but I sure am glad it happened. I had an incredible athletic director that was able to guide and point me in the right direction along the way. I look back and know how much I learned very quickly. I am definitely better for making those errors and learning the Get A Stop (G.A.S.) Mindset. Because of my experiences there and a good friend's encouragement, we went on to build a pretty special team with lifetime memories that I am thankful for every day.

- CHAPTER 2 -

SUCCESS IS ALIGNING HABITS WITH YOUR GOALS

I learned this expression a while ago, and I disagreed with it at the time. How can success be a choice? Some people have it and some people don't, right? First of all, I wish someone would have shared with me at that time that success is simply how you choose to measure it. It has nothing to do with how others see you or what the world defines as success. I learned very quickly that what constitutes success to one person may not be a success to another. One person's idea of success could be impacting other people's lives, while other people's definition could be building a family, or building a championship team. For others, it may be totally defined by a fancy title or how much money they can earn in a year.

I now believe and understand that before you can determine success or failure you must set the goal. This isn't something that should be loosely determined. Instead, setting the goal should be the priority. Set the goal and then align all of your habits toward that specific goal. If the goal is to retire early, then align your financial decisions and habits to hit the retirement age goal. If your goal is to be a head Division I coach, then align your daily habits and decisions toward it. This would include choosing which job to take and learning how to develop and implement your own coaching philosophy by the head coaches you work for during each stop.

My honest belief is that the majority of people in the world have no idea what their specific goals are each day. I've been there: you wake up and you follow the routine of what you've been doing. You haven't worked towards anything specific, and you just want to survive the day. To live with true purpose, you have to set goals. People are sometimes afraid to verbalize what their goals truly are.

Maybe because someone may think they are silly or criticize them or, even worse, laugh at their aspirations if they share their goals. Well, take the harshness of those options and still yell it from the mountain. Release the fear and move toward your goals and dreams.

If you want it, then speak it. Scream it! I want to win a national championship! I want a college degree! I want a huge family! I want to be a millionaire! It doesn't matter what your goal may be. It only matters that you are committed to it. Search your heart for what you want, and then align your life to get it. To really set goals, you have got to have time with yourself, know yourself and get to know what you truly want out of this one life. After all, you only get one to live. I am a big goal setter, but I am an even bigger planner in regards to reaching those goals.

> *Release the fear and move toward your goals and dreams.*

As a matter of fact, I designed the P3 (Pocket Production Planner), and it's available to download on the website (www.influenceandimpacters.com). This handy and simple organizational device has allowed me to rate and monitor the progress I make toward my goals. It starts by listing my affirmations, my to-do list, my 90-day goals, and my long-term goals. It's pretty obvious once it's on paper if your daily to-do lists do not match the 90-day goals. Then, it becomes even more obvious when your daily activity is not matching your long-term goals. Adjust, adjust, adjust! And adjust quickly. One major error happens when you decide to wait to adjust next Monday or January 1. It is important to acknowledge the error and quickly adjust.

Two common mistakes occur when you are not reaching your goals at the rate you expect. The first one is the inability to recognize misalignment of activity quickly enough. This could simply be by being tricked by what seems urgent. Two, you could be getting too bogged down in drama and issues which can distract you from your goals. This is actually the first concept I teach a team each season. Throughout this book, you will learn the three mindset lessons that I believe are key to success.

MINDSET LESSON #1:

SEE ISSUES AND DRAMA SIMPLY AS A DISTRACTION FROM THE GOAL

Let's get real with ourselves. It's time for a one-on-one, heart to heart. What do you want? Define success for yourself. When do you want it? How are you going to get it?

If you are still figuring out what you want, then I would suggest pausing and sitting with it for as long as it takes. Really get to your heart and then recognize that success is a choice! It is your choice. Set your goals and then align your daily habits to your goals.

MACYOLOGY:

SUCCESS IS A CHOICE

The Story

I woke up one morning and realized I was fat. I didn't see it coming and only realized it happened after my knees and body ached after each practice session. How in the world did this happen? It didn't happen after one cheeseburger, but it did happen after six months of bad habits. It hit me like a ton of bricks. I was not able to sustain great energy through a 3-hour training session and after the session, I was totally exhausted. I knew that at this rate I could not be an active coach with the kind of energy I required of myself, and the team would pay the price.

I immediately started coaching myself out of this hole. "Ok coach, listen to your own advice. Set the goal, design a plan, and now be disciplined enough to execute it." I came up with a plan that included four sets of 12 repetitions and 40 minutes of cardio: basically, a basketball game strategy for added mental motivation. I performed the routine every day and I saw no immediate results. However, I believed in the workout and was motivated by the designed strategy. Now, this wasn't some gimmick diet or professionally designed workout. It was simply something I believed in, completed consistently, and it provided significant numerical meaning to me.

After about three months, my clothes fit me a little bit more loosely. Then a few months after that, I felt amazing. I had dropped some weight, but more importantly, I had more energy, felt confident, and ready for the physical challenges that were ahead.

Make no mistake: I was frustrated during the process of weight loss and being on such a consistent schedule. When no one really acknowledged that physically I was experiencing changes or bragged on my consistency, it was pretty disappointing. I had to simply acknowledge to myself that I felt good about it and hoped eventually everyone else would be able to see the results of my hard work. I went to the gym and trained because I knew that consistency would win out in the end. I was motivated to do it even when I did not "feel" like doing it. My motivation was not only for my benefit. I knew that my team's success depended on my stamina as well.

The power of all my efforts was honestly that I personally and whole-heartedly believed in the plan. I knew physical endurance was required to have any longevity in the coaching profession. So, without a fuss, I stuck to the plan. I am so thankful I did. I felt better, had more energy, and was better for the players throughout that season. My energy level was at an all-time high. In addition, the team and my long-term health benefited.

I always assess my health toward the end of a basketball season. If I am low on gas by early March, I did a poor job of staying consistent. If I feel in peak shape mentally and physically for postseason play, I know I was more consistent with my habits. Positive habits for me during a season include not only exercise but also adequate sleep and proper hydration. It seems pretty simple, but it is a six-month test. From travel, game preparation, and high-stress levels, the challenge of having your habits match the initial goals and desired results is a large endeavor. Throughout this professional, health-related journey, I learned that success is truly a choice based upon the habits I committed to completing each day.

- CHAPTER 3 -

CONSISTENCY IS THE TRUEST MEASURE OF PERFORMANCE

W hat is the secret to success? Keep showing up! I know it sounds simple - way too simple - but I promise it works. Just keep showing up. In 7th grade, I read a quote, and it has stuck with me all of these years. It said in part, "Consistency is the truest measure of performance. Some people may be great for 30 minutes or even 30 days, but true success lies in the ability to do it day after day, week after week and year after year." For whatever reason, this really impacted me. As an athlete, I would have a good shooting night, and I would remember this quote. As a student, I would get a good grade and immediately remember this quote. It helped me as I prepared for the next game or test. It became a huge game of different ways to challenge myself to be consistently better each day. Just how consistent could I be? I see it as a huge compliment when anyone describes someone else as consistent. They may be consistently kind, brilliant, tough or demanding, but I can appreciate it. Can you?

Let me ask you a question: Are you a quitter? A quitter in your job, marriage, or team? Think about it. What have you quit in your life that you already regret? My quitting regret would be the Girl Scouts! Isn't that crazy? I remember quitting the Girl Scouts at a very young age. I'm not even sure why, but I'm mad that I did. We all know that life is consistently hard. We all know that challenges present themselves daily in

By pushing forward past what others may see as doom and failure is actually where success lies.

life. Why are we buying into society's concept that quitting is allowed? Why is it so easy to do? Quitting becomes the simple answer when things are not going your way. Look around. It's everywhere. It's a bad habit to start. Quitting builds no character, and it definitely does not build itself into a good old story of defying all odds later on in life.

During trials and hard times your brain will tell you to make a choice and here are your options: RUN - HIDE – QUIT. Which one will you choose? I read that the Navy Seals refer to it as flight, fight, or freeze. I love that! If you can acknowledge when that decision-making process is approaching, you can make a courageous choice. I'm definitely not saying that there's not a time to exit stage left, but I am saying there is way more success generally when you keep showing up and working toward the goal.

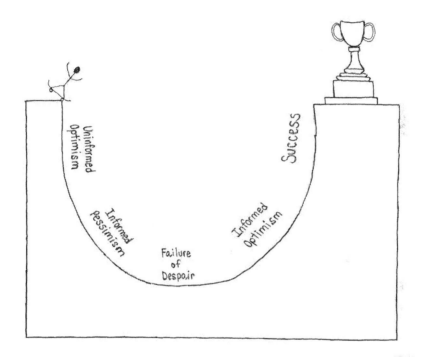

Check out this fun and simple reverse bell curve illustration. I read about it during one of the toughest losing streaks in my coaching career. This curve has always stuck with me during any dark time. By pushing forward past what others may see as doom and failure is actually where success lies. My major takeaway with it was that if you stop and start over this same process is going to restart and happen over again. It is painful, and most people stop before success has even had a chance to rise to the top. It will make the start over totally back breaking. Do not break prior to the breakthrough. I often remind myself of this fact. Pick something you are currently challenged with and acknowledge where you are along the bell curve. If you just keep going, can you make it to the next phase? If so, you are one step closer to reaching success. Pause before you make the decision to quit. We know that when we keep showing up that we are closer to consistency and it is the truest measure of performance.

MACYOLOGY:

KEEP SHOWING UP

The Story

Picture this one: a head Division I basketball coach at the age of 31. In my opinion, I was way too young and inexperienced for the expectations ahead. To say this was a daunting task for me would be an understatement. Everything was moving way too fast. It was kind of like a young player in their first college game: no matter what you do, you aren't emotionally catching up. Trust me, the game isn't slowing down, and the competition isn't waiting for you to catch up. Strategy one: fake it until you make it. Bad decision. Strategy two: make it everyone else's fault. Another bad decision. Strategy three: tell the truth, be vulnerable and ask for help. The right decision. The key for me was to align with solid, good-hearted people and to just keep going.

We were finally projected to have the team that made the NCAA tournament! We were loaded from top to bottom with talent and heart. We had offensive and defensive weapons all over the floor. I was as excited as I can ever remember to coach a team. Then, weird stuff started happening. One player was injured while at home. Another player was injured outside of practice. Another one at practice. Another one at a game. Then another one and another one. I mean honestly, stuff was happening that you just could not make up. How in the world could half of the team be out with season-ending injuries? I attempted to stay positive and remind myself that the seven players that we do have available are a very strong seven. I believed we could still get it done. Then, the failure continued to build and elevate. We would lose in the final possession once, twice, three times. We would miss free throws to seal games. We missed open shots to win games. It was a constant heartbreak.

What was I planning to do as the leader of this team of

athletes? I referred back to what I learned early in my process of being a Division I basketball coach. I reminded myself of the three choices I had to make, and I believe I got it right. I chose strategy three, and I told the truth. I said, "I do not know why these things are happening to our team." All I knew is that I wanted these young people to see a woman that was not making excuses and was not giving up. I referred to the reverse bell curve more than once that season. The media would make excuses for the losses and ask me to agree with it. Wow, that would have been easy to do, but then the example I set for the players would be wrong. For the rest of their lives, these kids would learn a terrible lesson. I could not bear to show that when something goes wrong you just make an excuse for it. So, I told the only truth I knew. Yes, we have had injuries and yes, we have been bad at the end of games and yes, these kids' hearts are breaking during this process, but there would be no excuses for it.

This season stands as the most heartbreaking of my entire career, but I do not regret the decision I made to endure and stay the course. I would define that season as one of many regrets. It holds true as an example for me of a season that I will not make excuses for, ever. At the end of that tough season, we did advance in the conference tournament and had our first ever WNBA player. I would say we elevated from the failure toward success.

- CHAPTER 4 -

EVENT VS. OPPORTUNITY

O ne of the greatest limits that we can put on ourselves is the inability to *SEE*. Not to see what is in front of us, but to truly see with the ability to *RECOGNIZE*. Too many times to count, I've seen only after the fact. I missed the vital opportunity to recognize while the experience was happening. If only I could have paused at that moment and said something differently, or even responded differently, then the impact of that moment would have been dramatically more positive.

My best solution to correct this issue is the concept of Event vs. Opportunity. The power comes in our ability to see opportunity in everything. Did you hear your iPhone ding? That's right, it is your next meeting, class or practice. Can you see that as a total opportunity? An opportunity to help, change, or impact someone else's experience or life? This may take being so in the present moment that you develop a new-found ability. It will be so impactful to you and everyone around you for a lifetime.

Life is bigger than your to-do list. Busy minds will prevent us from truly getting past seeing and into true recognizing. I get it. Life starts moving fast, and it is very difficult to recognize opportunity during those moments. It's during a transition or a stressful time that you need this reminder even more. Sometimes it is not even opportunity we don't recognize. Instead, it's the needs of the people that we love and care about the most. We become so caught up in our phones and computers that we lose touch with what really matters. I worked for a very smart man that once told me, "Heather, love things that can love you back." I know for sure the phone, computer, nor

Life is bigger than your to-do list.

the television will never love me back. It is a daily discipline to recognize when these moments come and go. It becomes a daily challenge not to miss one of these moments.

Next time your schedule becomes totally packed, allow that ding of your iPhone to be your quick reminder. Allow it to trigger your mind into recognizing the opportunity. To recognize who loves you and deserves your time. That small noise can now help you never miss the opportunity to impact and influence. Do you hear it? Opportunity is waiting for you.

MACYOLOGY:

LOVE IS ON THE GIVE, NOT ON THE TAKE

The Story

A few years ago, the concept of this book got started based upon an event vs. opportunity moment. I was asked to be a guest speaker in a graduate level leadership course on a Tuesday night at 6:00 p.m. Well, that is not exactly what I wanted to do at that time and I definitely did not see it as a wonderful opportunity. I resisted attending to the point of figuring out a solid excuse to decline the invite. I even attempted to decrease the time of my availability. My brain raced with ways to get out of the obligation.

Only because of the professor's persistence, I agreed to do a question and answer session for 20 minutes. Once I arrived, the professor said, "The class is yours." I started to panic because I only had 20 minutes of material prepared regarding the roles of managers compared to the roles of a leader. Of course, doubt started to creep into my mind. Insecurities from childhood started to show up and then I had to make that ever-important choice. Do you rise to the occasion or do you stumble through it?

I am very particular about any speaking opportunities I accept. When I was younger, I struggled with overcoming a speech impediment. I still feel like a kid every time I am in front of a group. I get nervous each and every time. To this day, regardless of the type of speaking event that I'm invited to attend, I always show up with butterflies. It could be 20 minutes at a school or an hour presentation to a Fortune 500 company. The best way to approach the anxiety for me has been through preparation. You can only imagine this event quickly turned into a defining moment for me. Fast forward one hour and that hour was one of my most rewarding visits inside the classroom. I was extremely thankful for an amazing group of students and, of course, long-winded storytelling. I was able to maximize my time in the class, and the students were engaging and inquisitive. I was thankful and energized walking out of the room.

I am still disappointed in myself for my initial negative attitude toward this opportunity. See, I only saw it as an event when I should have seen this as an opportunity to get outside of my comfort zone. It was an opportunity to give. I had a chance to be around bright students that had set goals to work within intercollegiate athletics. I hope in sharing my experiences that I helped those students with their future decisions and choices. More importantly, I know that I gave all I had in that hour to those students. However, that day, those students gave me more. I walked away with a million dollars' worth of energy!

I learned big-time lessons that day. One: never be too busy for what is truly important; and two: it's better to be over prepared rather than under prepared each and every time. Interestingly enough, the next day I received an email from the professor inquiring whether I had thought of writing a leadership book. Sometimes all you need is a little encouragement every now and then along with a bit of courage to get it started. Wow, what an idea and opportunity from simply a Tuesday night class. Never again will I make the mistake of not seeing everything I do in life as an opportunity.

- CHAPTER 5 -

DEFINING TOUGHNESS

How do you define toughness? There are hundreds of books written on the topic, and we all strive to define it in sports. Webster's Dictionary defines toughness as "being strong enough to withstand adverse conditions." What about you? How do you define it for yourself, team or organization?

After having coached for over 18 years, I can tell you that the word "tough" is actually overused like some muscles. You've got to be the toughest physically, and the most mentally tough person and team each night. I've heard it used so much that it's become sickening. Are you physically tough enough? Are you mentally tough enough? I decided at that point to do what I tend to do when something seems complex and overused. I came up with my own thoughts on it and how to positively maximize it within my life and circle of influence.

I believe that toughness is simply your ability not to rationalize. It's that simple. When you want to make an excuse, you don't rationalize it. When you want to understand, but you don't get why this or that happened or why someone said or did something, don't rationalize it. Do you want to be tough? Then, do not rationalize it. Let's figure out a solution, the next best action, and get to work. In my opinion, that takes real toughness.

When teams lose or the budget numbers are missed, then we need a reason, an excuse, and we need it quickly. The media, the fans, and your boss all want a reason. So, here we go down that road in our minds. The excuses in sports are always the easiest to find: new sets, better execution, and tougher practices. Listen, I could have used a multitude of these excuses during any season and many days

I wanted too, badly. Real life lessons are great teachers during these decisive moments. I've learned as a coach to live this toughness definition. To live the message. To be an example of what you want others to walk each day. I decided not to rationalize losing and never make an excuse. I learned that valuable lesson in the middle of failure. You just keep going and never rationalize the adversity.

And mostly you've got to figure out the reason you will stand tall and be tougher today than you were the day before. Maybe it is because all eyes are watching what toughness looks like from a coach, a woman, a mom, and a friend. Trust me, it is a great compliment to be described as "tough!"

Does it sound too simple or maybe like it won't work? I am excited to introduce the second team concept we learn each year with our team:

MINDSET LESSON #2:

YOU ARE THE CHIEF INTERPRETER OF YOUR OWN REALITY

Each day when events occur, you have a choice of seeing it as a negative or a positive. It's similar to what I describe to the team as a "Warrior Mindset." This is when you choose to see everything as a challenge. You make the choice to see what lies ahead as a positive and an opportunity, instead of seeing it as the world is against you and you are a victim. It will take a very tough-minded person to have this mindset. It is a learned skill and a powerful skill once mastered. I recognize that it is much more comfortable and acceptable to be the victim and to make excuses. However, the true freedom and happiness happen when you are in control of your own thoughts and perspectives.

Be tough, because you are the chief interpreter of your own life. Make the choice not to rationalize. Make a positive choice. Remember, after all, the opposite of tough is soft and who wants to be defined as soft?

MACYOLOGY:

TOUGHNESS IS YOUR ABILITY NOT TO RATIONALIZE

The Story

It's 6:00 a.m. and we are lifting weights in the pre-season. These are always the toughest training sessions for the team because it tests them not only physically but mentally. I decided that this would be a great opportunity to teach *MINDSET LESSON #2*. I walked in about mid-way through the training and simply stood and observed. I said very little to anyone and with very little expression. Gradually, I started to notice the players observing my demeanor and whispering. So, I kept up the act and even built it up a little. I adjusted my body language to show anger and disappointment.

As the training session came to an end and the team huddled, I casually walked into the huddle and said, "Meet me in the locker room." I could have said, "Get on the line" or, "You guys are in big-time trouble" and get the exact same response. It was like a

> *. . . true freedom and happiness happen when you are in control of your own thoughts and perspectives.*

black cloud of negativity took over the team. As we made the walk towards the locker room it was total silence. I was sure everyone was thinking, "Who did it this time?" The walk over seemed to take forever and you could feel the nervous anxiousness. When we finally made it to the locker room, I simply started going over our weekend announcements like normal. The players all looked around totally surprised, shocked and a little confused.

This was the perfect real-life example to illustrate and talk in depth about *MINDSET LESSON* #2 within the context of our program. I dove deep into the concept of what being a chief interpreter really looks like to live in a more positive state. Everyone in the room made the choice to go negative. Everyone in the room had the choice to make that morning. We control our own responses. The choice to perceive me as being upset, mad, or negative was their choice. Everyone could have made the decision to interpret my behavior differently, more positively. As human beings, we tend to always lean toward the negative. Why not interpret my behavior as, "Coach is definitely not a morning person" or, "I hope coach is doing ok and not going through something tough personally" or, "Good morning, Coach. How's it going?"

I described the event and the reality of what happened, and the team all began to laugh and agree that they chose to interpret my behavior as negative. I went a step more in teaching how to have a "Warrior Mindset." When a coach says the phrase, "Get on the line," athletes know it is about the dreaded conditioning session. It's similar to the boss saying, "We need to meet" and seeing it as a bad sign. I challenged each of them to see "Get on the line" as a warrior would see the challenge ahead. To have this mindset, an athlete must see it as, "Okay, great. I'm getting on the line to be in better shape than everyone else, and I will be a better athlete when game time comes." This is when we learned to run each sprint as a warrior rather than with a loser and victim mindset.

I think that embracing the challenge of being the true *chief interpreter* of your own reality allows you to choose to be positive and not waste precious time worrying about the worst-case scenario. Typically, the worst-case scenario never actually happens or at least it only happens at a very low percentage of the time. When we are able to live life as I learned to live during EQ training as a "chief interpreter" and with a "warrior mindset," then it becomes much clearer on how to recruit positive emotions in our lives. With these mindsets as the foundation, you will not rationalize. You will define toughness.

In the Bonus Section, learn more about Emotional Intelligence and my experience of becoming EQ certified. The chapter, "My EQ Journey," is located in the back of the book.

- CHAPTER 6 -
HARD WORK

I f I was asked to write a letter to the one element or trait in my life that has equaled the most success, then it would start something like this:

Dear Hard Work,

THANK YOU. Nothing gets accomplished that is worth accomplishing without you included. You can call yourself something different or dress yourself up differently, but ultimately there is no substitute for you. I am a firm believer that you, hard work, can make up for many, and sometimes all, deficiencies. Combining you, hard work, with a high level of competency, makes for a combination that leads to greatness. So again, thank you, hard work. I could not have done anything without you. I owe you everything and without you, I am nothing.

Two Feet In with You, ALWAYS,
~ Heather

I know that sounds kind of silly, but I think that hard work has gotten a bad name. Let's get this cleaned up and get it all sorted out now. The words "hard work" are not dirty words. However, hard work has become a scary thought or phrase to some people. It is also what some people run from and at times, want to get totally away from when making decisions.

I believe it to be a fact that no one wants to be called lazy. Well, couldn't the opposite of hard work be laziness? All day, every day, I want to be described as hard working. I want to take on challenges that will require hard work. And I want to be pushed, so when I lie down at night, I know that I gave all I had and feel a sense of accomplishment and satisfaction. I refuse to run when the hard work starts. I actually tend to run toward the toughest challenge and the project that will require an intense level of hard work to get it done. This is where the fun lies.

The recognition that embracing hard work and actually running toward the challenge of hard work is where satisfaction is waiting. When something is hard, then I know without a doubt that in the long run, it is going to be totally worth it. If this sounds tough, scary or even counter-cultural to you, then keep reading. This is not about me being right and you being wrong. This is all about alignment and like-mindedness. The alignment with whom you choose to associate with regarding work ethic, values, and beliefs must be the same. Without this alignment, the elevation of conflict will escalate quickly. The like-minded trait of hard work will produce a strong unbreakable culture. This will become a connection within the entire group that can always be a point to re-center and reunite if the group gets off track.

> *The like-minded trait of hard work will produce a strong unbreakable culture.*

So, don't run from hard work and don't dodge it because you must live it to get what you want. Do you want that big beautiful home? Work for it. Do you want the job promotion? Work for it. Do you want a great relationship with your kids? Work for it. I have a strong personal belief that with hard work I can accomplish anything.

MACYOLOGY:

THE PRICE OF ADMISSION

The Story

Our team got good. Really good! The better we got, the more I wanted. I've always been told that my own ambition would be my eventual downfall. I have a constant desire for more, and I push for more all of the time. I'm not sure where I got this from or how to get rid of it. It drives people around me kind of nutty, and it drives me so hard that it keeps me up at night. It's the idea that if I'm not working, then someone is, and when I meet them, they will beat me. I think as an athlete I always felt this to be true, and it pushed me. I know that I never want to be in a situation where in my gut I know that I am not 100% prepared. The key point here is that *I* need to know that *I* am 100% ready, and it does not matter if others feel this way. *I must feel this way.* I am driven toward the need to be satisfied, and I am rarely, if ever truly satisfied.

This story starts like this: imagine growing a program so fast that you outgrow your recruiting talent. Imagine growing a program so fast that you outgrow your athletic department's budget. Imagine growing so fast that you couldn't pay your coaches enough to retain them through the success the team was experiencing. I saw this coming, and the train was going so fast that I didn't know how to stop it. I foreshadowed what was coming our way, but the resources just were not there to prevent the brick wall that was going to eventually hit us. So, I controlled what I could control, put my head down, and kept my foot on the pedal.

To continue to succeed, I adjusted. The first adjustment was the approach toward recruiting, and that's where the mistakes started. I began recruiting "different" coaches and that then resulted in recruiting "different" athletes. These folks had talent, and I mean ultra-amounts of God-given talent around the game of basketball. When I would sit back and watch them walk into the gym, I would just say, "WOW!" They walked with a certain level of confidence and sureness. I was impressed. I was thrilled to be around such talent daily. I was excited and thrilled until I learned the hard truth. The hard truth was that all of these individuals did not have anything to bond them together. Each team needs a *why* to stay on track during the good and, more importantly, through the bad times. I believe the really special teams have glue that holds them all together. The magic glue for us had always been hard work. This is a universal commitment and something that we all have in common regardless of where we are from or what we believe.

When I adjusted the term "hard work" within our recruiting it was a calculated error. Instead of calling hard work what it really is, I called it "good work." Now that sounded wonderful for a while, but then we got started, and I realized that was way too misleading. I'm pretty creative and a risk taker, so why not call it, "different work?" That's it. We'll call it different. Because it really is different. I am a recruiter after all, and that sounded sexy and I knew it would sell. It did a great job on the attraction, but not on the retention. Once the coaches and players bought into the "different work" concept but arrived to "hard work" it was like, "Wait a minute. This isn't what I signed up for." "Yikes," I thought to myself. This group was interested in different work but definitely not interested in hard work.

It was a talented group, yes, but not a group of hard workers. The thought of maximizing the talent with combining working hard was impossible for them to swallow. We had misalignment within the group. I had gone away from one of the three program standards. Hard work had always been a standard and it was non-negotiable. I could have kicked myself for reshaping what is never a corner that can be cut.

I had to make a tough decision for the long-term betterment of our program. I knew we had amazing players with no interest in what we are offering. My first action was to apologize for dressing up the recruiting speech. I asked for forgiveness and then asked if they could conform to our program standards in the short term. If at the end of the season they wanted to join a new team, then I would support it. But from that day forward no one stayed in our program that was not willing to work hard and live by the standards. I knew in my heart that many people in that room would be unable to do it long term. I made the choice that I was willing to watch the talent walk out of the gym to get the culture corrected. We were interested in the best players that wanted to work for everything they got. They would work hard for themselves but also work hard for the team. It was hard to see many of them go, but it was worth it to see the ones who chose to stayed flourish. Some players left that year, and some stayed to see their habits and lives changed forever.

I learned the greatest lesson that season. The *Price of Admission* to be a part of our program will always be hard work. However, recruiting the truth and determining the blueprint is first. Once it is established, then there is zero compromise, ever. I am proud of being demanding. I am all in with every possession with no let-up, ever! It is different, and I refuse to apologize for it. Well, I found that a major key is that all coaches and players must clearly know what they have signed up for because this way isn't for everyone. We will always stay the course. We now know that when you combine a high level of competency with an incredible work ethic, no one or nothing is stopping that train.

- CHAPTER 7 -

THE BEST TEACHER IS OTHER PEOPLE'S EXPERIENCES

From a young age, I always heard the saying that the best lesson is, "Learn from other people's experiences." This is valuable advice. Why do we not pay closer attention to this advice? There's no greater teacher than a person with experience. I wish I would have listened more to my parents and older sister. When you know that person has your best interest at heart and loves you more than they love themselves, then you need to remove your ego and listen. I specifically mention family, but it could be a teacher, coach, or mentor. The key is removing the doubt of the other person's motives. To listen and act on solid advice, you must know that that person loves and wants the best for you regardless of the circumstance.

I think we all can have some skepticism and doubt when it comes to following advice. Can I really trust that this person wants the best for me? If I follow this advice, will this person have something to gain? We need to adjust our thinking or adjust the person from whom we choose to ask for advice in this circumstance. One technique I've used is to look into the eyes of the person sharing a story or a life lesson and see their heart. If I can see their heart, then I mostly make the choice to listen. I have also learned to listen to part of the lesson. I have a technique of filing it away in a specific category, so I am ready to pull it back out when it is needed.

My hope is that you will take my advice and listen to the people who have been awarded that t-shirt. I definitely choose to go on my own adventure more than I listened to other's experiences. I was, in some cases, very hard-headed and decided to learn on the fly. I made big mistakes along the way. I learned the best offense in the country and was told by the teacher that the type of athlete I wanted to recruit wasn't smart enough to learn it. I didn't listen and went on to win, win and win some more with the formula. I was told by a professional consultant not to hire this or that assistant coach. I didn't listen and went on a sad and drama-filled journey of misalignment. Half of the time I didn't listen to the ones that had the *t-shirt* of experience. Sometimes it worked out beautifully, and it's a great story. The other half of the time when I picked incorrectly, it was life-altering. Again, listen to the ones that you trust and that have more experience, especially if there has been a success in that area. If you can pick it right 70% of the time, then you'll win more than you will lose.

A challenge now becomes taking away what you can in each situation and being willing to leave the rest. If you are listening to someone that already has the life experience of success, then pay attention. If your advice is coming from someone that has already run the 5K, won the conference championship, wrote the book, been there on vacation or even lost a loved one, then take the time for the feedback. There are lessons to learn from everyone in every situation, but we can never make one person's opinion and their direction the end all. Without a doubt, pay attention if they've already won big

It may go wrong, it may go right, but either way, it is going and so are you.

or lost even bigger. I always say that if you want to do what someone else has already done, then ask them how they got there and take the short route.

Take the data in, listen to your gut, and jump. It may go wrong, it may go right, but either way, it is going and so are you. After all, the key is always adjusting quickly and having fun.

MACYOLOGY:

PAY ATTENTION WHEN THEY ALREADY HAVE THAT T-SHIRT

The Story

My mom told me: "Get a real job. Learn a trade. You'll always have a job that is needed. Something like a nurse or a teacher. Whatever you do, do NOT become a coach! In coaching, there is no way to make a decent living or life." Basketball has always been my passion. If staying around it meant I needed to coach multiple sports and teach in the classroom, then it is what I planned to do. At this point and time, my success was going to be working as many jobs as possible to get to coach college basketball. In the back of my mind I thought if I could just earn $40,000 doing it, I had made it!

My mom's advice was good advice from someone that loved me and did not want me to struggle with how harsh life can be. It was good advice to be conservative. I cannot fault her for the advice from her perspective, and to this day I thank her for the advice. She knew her daughter and knew my drive. From a young age, if you told me I could not accomplish something, then I wanted it even more. I'm still not sure if she meant to utilize reverse psychology, but it worked like magic.

I went on an incredible journey to prove her wrong and make her proud all at the same time. I played two college sports (basketball and tennis) just in case I would need to be prepared to coach multiple sports to realize my dream. I also went on to get a master's degree to be prepared to teach and earn a salary to survive while I was enjoying my passion of coaching college basketball. After only five years as an assistant coach, I was able to get a head coaching job at the college level. I finally did it and proved my mom wrong. It honestly just felt okay. I learned that was not my true goal or final success. My success would come by accomplishing my long-term dream of becoming a Division I head coach. It took me another five years, but I finally did it. Thankfully enough, to get to this accomplishment so quickly I did it by listening and taking coaching. In my case, I was pushed by doubt and pulled by a desire for half of the goal. However, I needed both to accomplish my true, scary, big dream of doing it at the highest level.

- CHAPTER 8 -

PERSEVERANCE ON YOUR JOURNEY

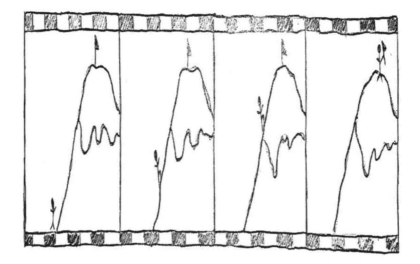

O ne of the greatest attributes a person can possess is their ability to persevere. It is the toughest thing sometimes to wake up each morning and continue on step by step. One more day, one more hour, one more minute in some cases. The attribute of perseverance tests the true character of a human being. Life's struggles are real: jobs, relationships, and the ever-changing landscape of events that occur. We all anticipate that conflict and struggles will happen in our life, but are we preparing each day for our response to it? I would argue that most people just worry that it will happen and hope it doesn't. The people that bounce back from adversity the fastest are the people that prepare for the proper response when adversity hits. Those people have the true genius in life mastered.

MINDSET LESSON #3:

ELITE PERFORMERS LEAVE NOTHING TO CHANCE, EVER.

When in preparation, one of the vital elements is preparing for those times when mishaps or adversities strike. This is when you have given thoughtful consideration of elements within an equation, and you are better prepared emotionally when the actual decision-making event happens. I should say *when* and *if* the event actually ever occurs. This could simply mean packing an extra pair of headphones on a road trip, reviewing your notes one final time prior to an exam, or formulating multiple solutions when the big sales pitch gets rejected. But regardless, being an elite performer means leaving nothing to chance, and I mean nothing.

In athletics, the word "perseverance" is easy to see. You can spot it when athletes are recovering from an injury or when a coach is turning a program around and it seems like it will never make that turn. The beauty occurs when we can see four frames ahead. This technique will enable us the ability to bounce back quicker. It is when we get surprised or something sneaks up on us that it can take way too long to get back up. This is especially true after we get the breath knocked out of us. Part of being a great athlete is seeing ahead of the possession to anticipate the next action as opposed to always reacting. A great coach is uncannily good at this in game time situations. It's like a magician. I have seen it over and over again: the great ones see several frames ahead and make the games more anticipatory than reactionary. I also think this skill makes for great leaders.

The trait of perseverance combined with the understanding of how to be an elite performer is a formula for recovering from a set back stronger than ever.

The trait of perseverance combined with the understanding of how to be an elite performer is a formula for recovering from a set back stronger than ever. Trust me when I say the key to a setback is the bounce back. Can you think of a situation in your life where you needed to step outside the frame to see the full picture? Don't you think that if you could have done that faster, then the disaster could have been avoided? If you can predict and anticipate, then you are able to act with more confidence and precision. It sometimes feels like you've already been there when you get very good at it. One great decision-making technique is to stay ahead of the elements by processing the potential mishap. What are three possible outcomes? If each of the three occurs, what is your decision or action? Regardless of what may or may not happen, you are prepared. It may be tough, but you will be strong and ready to bounce back. I want to be defined as an *ELITE* performer, so I make the choice each day to leave nothing to chance, ever.

MACYOLOGY:

IT'S ABOUT YOUR BOUNCE BACK ABILITY

The Story

I know I can get this thing right, I just know I can! But, I have been notorious for being a bad picker. We can even reflect back to when I was a kid. I'd pick the wrong team during a game in PE class, the wrong classmates to work with on an assignment in class and even the wrong prom date. I figure it is mostly because I always see someone's potential. Well, you know what they say about potential?

Anyway, now it is my big opportunity. I have finally accomplished my long-term goal and it is time to lead. One of the major responsibilities of being a head coach is to put a team together. With time, I became pretty good at picking the athletes. I mean, after all, 70% of it is athletic skills that you can see with your own eyes. The other 30% gets tricky sometimes. Remember now, I am a recruiter at heart, so I tend to sell more than I listen. If I got a head nod that a player was competitive and was willing to work hard, then I started to move the process forward. Sometimes, I moved it quickly when the athletic ability matched the answer to my question. Well, I am proud to say that we have built some really incredible teams on the court this way.

Now, the team behind the team is much more complicated. The formula we utilize in selecting athletes does not work the same as selecting a staff. Let's dive into this a little deeper. I have recognized a lot about myself during the selection process. Number one, I am a recruiter. Number two, I am a believer. And number three, I am optimistic that everyone is a truth-teller. It is natural, I think, to want to see the best in people. I want to believe that what you say, you will actually do. And I want to help people get better jobs and opportunities for their families because that feels good. This emotion definitely made me love hiring quickly.

With me being a natural recruiter, I have attracted good candidates over the years. I have hired and fired some really accomplished coaches, at least on paper, and I have been applauded by administrators about whom I could attract for the low salaries available. I feel fortunate to have worked with some amazing coaches, and I have learned so much from each of them. I also have taken full responsibility for the times when I got it wrong. Listen, I have definitely gotten it wrong. When I picked wrong, it didn't just hurt me. It hurt the group of coaches on the staff when that person underperformed and underdelivered. It hurt the players when that coach's competency was lacking. And more importantly, it hurt that person. I am sure it was frustrating to not be able to perform and deliver each day and to actually help a team be successful.

Half of the time when I was guilty of hiring incorrectly, that person was not ready for the challenge. Some of the time, they were just the right person at the wrong time. I believe there are some coaches that are great at blending in and coasting when the team is on top and there are some coaches that can help you climb from the bottom. The key is finding the coach that is equipped to help the team during the stage where the program is sitting at the time. Then, there became an art in helping that coach find a new challenge once the team matures into the next stage. I think it is a major turnoff to be around jaded, wounded and negative people, especially coaches. Well, the hiring and firing process can produce major scars that can start that process for anyone, I suppose. No one wants to be bad at their jobs and hate their boss, right? Again, I take full responsibility for the ones that I have gotten wrong, and I regret more than I can ever explain plenty of my decisions. Some good advice that I should have followed more: hire slow and fire fast.

I have two things that I am most thankful for during the journey of putting together a staff. The first and most important one is that I showed mercy and grace. The second one is that when I needed help, I was not too prideful to ask for it. There were many times when I had the green light to fire coaches on the spot, and I didn't because I knew how it would affect their families and their next job. There were many days I was angry and had grounds to make immediate staff changes, but I decided to show mercy and grace in those defining moments. I paid for it, but my heart will never regret attempting to do what was right for someone else. When I asked for help in selecting a staff, it was a real game changer. The consultant helped guide me in the process and became a sounding board that was invaluable. This entire process included making sure I knew the right questions to ask, holding me accountable for listening, and then putting those people into the right roles.

Through my failures, I have also found great personal success in formulating a staff. It was more rewarding than I could ever describe working each day alongside many of my former players. The passion and like-mindedness allowed us to accomplish more in a quicker amount of time. We were also having a blast working together to get it done. It was exactly what a team is supposed to feel and look like. I will always walk with my head held high that I got that one right, finally. I also feel the need to interject into this story that as many times as I have lost battles, I ultimately won the war. I won the war because my two lifelong best friends came out of all of this hiring mess. Are you kidding me? I have two forever friends when most people would just love to have one. We were able to work alongside one another for years. It's pretty cool to be with your best buddies each day, all day. We lived through the good seasons and cried through the bad ones. They have been like an extended family to me. It was more than I could have ever asked for in some of life's toughest situations. So, even with all of the bad picks I've had along the way, I sure did pick it right twice. You guys are my victories. So, in the end, I am the winner.

- CHAPTER 9 -

BE GENTLE, HIGH ACHIEVERS AND PERFECTIONISTS

A ttention! Attention! I am talking right to you guys. Yes, each of you Type A personalities. Do you consider yourself a perfectionist and a high achiever? Then you need to pay even closer attention to the wonderful advice I always ignored. Listen up now because I am talking right to you: be gentle. I heard these words, but I didn't listen. I was told this advice and I had it explained to me, and I even knew in my gut it was true. It is important, and it is a part of growth and development that I had never truly considered. Give yourself permission: permission to have fun, relax, learn what you love, and learn what gifts you have to give to this world.

I have been driven and a high achiever since I was a young kid. I can remember being in first grade and designing a plan to be prepared for the Saturday morning co-ed basketball league that started in fourth grade. Oh yes, I own it. I actually was preparing for a fourth-grade league three years in advance. I would dribble and shoot a ball all summer when other kids were swimming in the pool. I was urgent even at this young age. I can remember thinking that I only have three years, so I have to train hard now to be ready. I am who I am, but I have so much more to learn.

My life had always been so busy with the next problem to solve, phone call to make, film to watch, and practice to plan that I had no idea what space would feel like without all of these tasks to fill it. So, I learned to sit with it and figure out things I really enjoy and not just the things I am supposed to enjoy. I enjoy the softer things in my life: my puppy; a hot cup of tea; a warm blanket; talking to a good friend; a hard workout; a day trip to the beach; a visit with my family. What in the world? I am as intensely driven as anyone. Maybe I didn't know really who I was without a title and a meeting to attend. After I learned to give myself permission, I learned that I really like myself. No, actually I really love myself.

We are sometimes so busy making the next plan to do more, more, and even more, that we leave zero space in our lives. Space for what? Space to slow down and see what fills that space. By building in margins for what the day has in store, it can open up new experiences and relationships. In our current society, we earn a badge of honor for filling our schedules with meetings and more work. I was an expert at doing this. Realize that it is acceptable and even needed to build margin into your schedule and life each day. The entire day does not need to be filled with meetings and appointments. Trust that the empty space on your iPhone calendar is a positive thing. The discipline of choosing not to fill the margin with surfing social media will work. And saying "no" to the next invitation could allow your space to fill with a positive and exciting new adventure.

So, I learned to be gentle a little late in life. I am thankful for this lesson. Truth be told, I'm still learning it. It's a hard habit to break, and it's hard to say no to people, obligations, and expectations. Like with everyone, sometimes I fall back into it and other times I am great. Either way, I have given myself permission to just be still and gentle. It's okay to have an open afternoon to try something new or to have a mini adventure. Everything does not have to be perfect to be effective.

Like with most defining moments, we typically have a "big hurt" that helps us recognize it. I've had a lot of big hurts in my life and big lessons learned. Particularly, the defining moment that helped allow me to give myself permission to live and take time for myself was while our basketball team was experiencing one of the most successful periods in program history. It was hard to see quickly because success was happening all around me, but I was dying inside. Right in the middle of unparalleled success, all of a sudden - which we all know wasn't really all of a sudden - I felt exhausted. Not tired, but exhausted. There needs to be a larger word to help define what I felt during this time, but I'm pretty basic, so that's the best I've got. Looking back, I realize that maybe it was what some people define as burn out. All I know is that a good night's sleep didn't work. A nap didn't energize me, and many days I had to coach myself out of bed. How could this be happening right now when we have momentum? In hindsight, I believe it was happening because I never allowed myself to celebrate the good stuff. I never gave myself permission to retreat and treat myself to a break. After every goal that we set was accomplished, I just kept saying, "Next one." Nothing was ever enough. If I made one recruiting call, then I needed to make another one. If two booster events were scheduled that week, then the next week I wanted three. Once we sold 500 season tickets, then I wanted to sell 1,000 the next season. There was never the pause and celebration after the accomplishment was achieved. Nothing ever became enough for me, ever. Every day, I wanted more. The fact I wanted more caused me to push harder. Not just myself, but everyone around me. After 15 years of it, I finally hit the wall. This was my defining moment and the big hurt that taught me the best forever lesson.

Listen to me now: cut yourself a break and take care of you. I learned a huge lesson in what I now know is not being lazy or selfish. I wanted so badly to accomplish my goals and to exceed expectations that it became a way of life. During that season, I should have been having the most fun and enjoying life. Instead, I was miserable. Miserably tired, moody, and a little depressed. The team thankfully achieved, but I had no gas in the tank to help them if they needed me. I regret it very much. Thankfully, I was able to fight and conquer this challenge without the team suffering significantly. I learned a valuable lesson during a successful time for our team. The outside world was seeing what looked like a perceived success, but every day internally it was a failure.

I believe especially as women and female leaders, we must allow ourselves to take care of our needs first. By doing this, we will in fact be better and stronger for everyone that truly needs us. This can be counter-cultural, but you must be strong enough to do it. If your motivation to make this adjustment is to be your best for everyone around you, then do it. The ones that need us the most really need us to have a clear head and heart. This will allow us to give solid advice, to listen intently, and to not be so busy to not love them at that moment.

So, to the high achiever: this is your permission slip. Go get ice cream. Give a high five. Take a day off. Celebrate the smallest of victories. Enjoy this roller coaster ride and ride it with your hands in the air, screaming and smiling.

MACYOLOGY:

GO GET ICE CREAM

The Story

"For the hundredth time, I CARE! Why would I work so hard if I don't care? Why would this team come before everything else in my life if I don't care? What do you mean I only care about winning? I love you guys. I hold you accountable. I discipline you. I teach you how to work hard. How can you think I don't care? Let me scream this at you until you believe it." I repeated these words year after year and continued to receive the same feedback. But I care. It does not matter if no one else understands that fact. As long as I know what's in my heart and my intent, then I will accept the critical incorrect feedback.

One of the best ways I learned to show my care level was through quality time and constantly verbally reminding the people around me of my strong belief. I can remember that we were in the middle of preparing for the NCAA tournament. One of our best shooters had been in a major slump, and I mean a major slump. We had lost in the conference tournament finals but knew we were a favorite if she knocked down open shots. She had put so much pressure on herself in the weeks leading up to the game, that by this point she was miserable and not enjoying the final stretch of her senior season. You could see the frustration on her face. The fear of missing the next shot was causing her anxiety. I did all I knew to do at the time, which was spend extra time shooting with her in the gym. With enough hard work and repetition, then she could climb out of the slump and be good, right? Well, she shot repetition after repetition, and the hole got bigger and bigger. Eventually, she was even crying after the games we won if she shot 0-5 behind the three-point line. I am thankful for a point guard that put this teammate first and had a high level of empathy. The point guard called me. "Hey coach," she said, "You wanna make a national championship game or what?" I said, "Of course I do. Why?" She replied, "Well, you better sit down and talk to our shooter. Don't you see it? She just needs to know you still believe in her." I said, "Wait, what? This will cure her shooting slump?" She said, "Maybe. I don't know. But you've tried everything else."

So, I made a call and said, "Let's go have dinner together!" We ate her favorite meal and just talked. I mean, we talked about everything: some hoops, some family, some school, some relationship stuff. We laughed and cried and for me, it's one of the best memories during our time together. I felt more connected to her as an amazing person than I did as a kid that wasn't shooting well. I believe she walked away knowing how much I cared about her and not how much I cared about her jump shot. She laughed more and practiced better the following week. She played like a senior in the NCAA tournament. She was incredible! We didn't quite make the national championship game, but we did make the Sweet 16 and she was a HUGE reason why. Bigger than that, her final memories as a college basketball player were filled with success. I still owe that point guard a ton of gratitude because without her encouragement the ending of this story could have been very different. We all need good teammates in life and people that are willing to tell you the truth. The truth can sometimes come in very different ways. I am thankful for this experience and lesson. The answer may not be having ice cream or eating your favorite dinner, but we all need someone to look us in the eye and say, "I care about you."

- CHAPTER 10 -

REMOVE THE TRY AND THE EXIT STRATEGY

Aligning yourself with people and organizations without having an exit strategy is key. What does this mean? Well first, if your entire team has a plan B, then no one is working very hard for plan A to be successful. When you build your group with people who are committed to this project, this university, or this family, then they will find a way to make it work. I always think that "find a way" people are the best kind. Otherwise, they find a way to get out, to get around, or to get even.

One of the greatest illustrations of this is the famous concept of "burn the boat" *(if you haven't read the information or watched the videos, a quick google search is worth your time).* When you find there is nothing to run back to, then you wake up and work differently. You even walk into the front door of that day differently. "This is going to work out," you will say. You will think, "It is going to be successful, or it is not over until we are successful." When you align yourself with people that have no plan B or exit strategy, then you will see a different type of working hard and focus each day. The passion that goes into it is obvious, and you can feel it. I love being around people who are in their dream job or married to their heartthrob. You can see it in their eyes. The look is that there is just no way that this is not going to work out. Now, that is not to say it is happy trails every day, but it does give us all hope. Think of it like this: you wouldn't really want to marry someone that says, "If this doesn't work out exactly as I had planned, then I've got other options lined up." This is scary in the realm of marriage, but within teams, it could be just as scary.

When I have had the most success in recruiting, it happened when I didn't have to convince anyone to join the team and buy into the culture we were building. When there was already a high level of desire to be a part of the school, community, or program then it always worked out better. When someone wants to be there, then they will already be more positive and less likely to jump ship at the first sign of an issue. Typically, when you spend your time convincing people how good things will be, the doubt sets in very quickly when the rocky waters come storming in. The next step will start the process of formulating the exit strategy in their minds.

I've learned that alignment and like-mindedness are vital not only for successful and high performing teams but also for a balanced order in a group. Typically, the leader has zero exit strategy and if they do, then it's going to fail regardless. When you notice the leader's commitment, it will breed the same commitment. Leadership is demonstrated at the top. So, as the leader builds the group, alignment within the mindset is vital. Once the alignment occurs and the mission is outlined, then the activity to support the goal starts. If you find there seems to be unusual storming, then look around the group. How many have a built-in exit strategy? It may be time to have the "burn the boat" conversation to allow your team to accelerate.

> *Leadership is demonstrated at the top.*

A huge key for us was forming a group of like-minded coaches that were also overachievers. Coaches that demand excellence and coaches that are positive with a strong belief system will be magnets towards these exact types of players. One by one, day by day, you live out what overachieving looks like and you confront anything that appears average. Then you remove it from the thoughts and words of everyone within the team.

When we lost a game by a point, we stopped applauding the valiant effort. Actually, we became so serious about it that we removed the word "try" from our program. We learned that to "try" is to simply give yourself permission not to do it! We all decided that we were either going to get it done or not get it done, but no one was walking into our team with a "just try it out" attitude. This was an absolute game-changing decision. We got better in recruiting, and we got better in our accountability during games.

Some organizations will achieve goals early and often and many will get better opportunities due to this fact. When teams win or recruit really well, then typically coaches get offered new and larger opportunities. All of this is wonderful; however, I do strongly believe that if you can keep pushing and keep everyone urgent on the team's mission, then everyone will reach even larger goals together. Most of the time, we aren't willing to demonstrate patience long enough to allow this process to take place. I think it's because society is caught up in a microwave of success. Fans and alumni want to win. Investors want to see their funds grow faster quicker. Typically, if everyone can stick to the plan, then the winning will happen and when it happens it will happen bigger for longer and the investments will grow more than ever imagined.

If we could all remember that when we reach individual goals each day, then ultimately the group can reach huge long-term goals. Remove your individual group's exit strategy. Commit to something bigger than yourself and enjoy the ride.

MACYOLOGY:

WE ARE GREAT BECAUSE WE ARE URGENT

The Story

I've led a basketball team where the expectations were incredibly low. The entire community and area seemed to enjoy the concept of surviving within mediocrity. It was applauded to do your best and come up short. This was actually what had become the expectation, and I despised it. The fight was on, and I knew this was going to be a tough one.

The first challenge was to figure out how to combat what was being said outside of the athletic arena. As a coaching staff, we were working with a team to achieve excellence and the right mindset for a maximum of four hours a day when everyone around the team was supporting the motto of, *"Just try really hard"* for the other 20 hours of the day. We started fighting this fight head-on by addressing it with the team. I explained very directly to the team what I felt was going to become an issue as the season progressed and for some of the players as their careers progressed. I knew that this team could possibly overachieve and exceed everyone's expectations. I also knew that the outside noise could start to get loud. I wanted to make the players aware of the trap before they fell into it. I explained to them, "You'll go out to eat or you'll go shopping and you will be recognizable." My initial challenge to the players was to say, "Those people do not know you and do not know what we are doing each day, so do not allow them to have an opinion." My next piece of advice was to avoid social media surfing and newspaper articles. I would always remind them, "You are never as good as they say you are. You are also never as bad as they say you are."

As more and more practices and games were under our belts, we all knew this was a different type of team. The urgency felt very different. We started to get national recognition by receiving Top 25 votes, and we set many program records. Some players had already prepared and handled the success well, while others did not take our initial meeting seriously enough. They would come to me and say, "Coach, why did this person say this to me?" Or, "Coach, why would they tell me I should shoot less and pass the ball to her more?" Feelings were getting hurt, and our brains started to shift to external factors. We started to value other's opinions way too much. I reminded the team once again to shut out the noise. I reminded them that we will be a great team this season and we are great because we are urgent. Being urgent would mean committing to not making an excuse for the lack of mental preparation. The same level of physical preparation required equal attention to the mental side of success.

The final strategy was the biggest game changer. As previously explained, we removed the word "try" from our program's vocabulary. Initially, our staff removed the word from our vocabulary first and more importantly, our minds. I knew it was important for the coaches to be on board and set an example for the team. I mean after all, if we are unable to live it, how could we expect the players to do it? So, we stopped saying, "I'll try to get all of the recruiting calls made tonight." Or, "I'll try to swing by and handle it today." We said confidently to one another, "I will get all of the recruiting calls made tonight. I will swing by and handle it today." This not only changed what we actually got accomplished, but I saw our confidence elevate. We were able to hold one another accountable, and it turned into a fun game. By the time we introduced it to the team, it was second nature to us. The team got it! We were not going to *"TRY"* in our program. Either you do it or you don't. And we did it a whole lot more than we didn't mostly because we became urgent on our journey.

As a matter of fact, this was the season that we formulated our program's blueprint. We put on paper our program standards and core values. One of the agreed-upon core values was actually, "We are great because we are urgent." We demonstrated our urgency each day through small adjustments such as, talking directly about our concerns to one another and obviously by adjusting our vocabulary.

A strong culture is built not only by drawing up a blueprint but also by staying the course. The people with no exit strategy got it done that season. With no exit strategy in mind, we exceeded expectations.

- CHAPTER 11 -

DEFINING DISCIPLINE

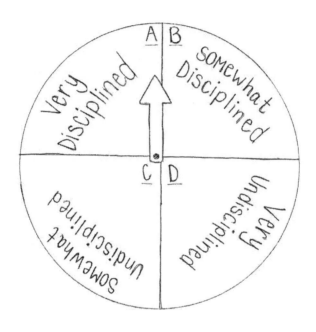

I have always been told that discipline is not something you do to people. Discipline is something you do for people. Without question, I believe that to be the case. When lacking a high level of discipline, very few things will get accomplished. Actually, well-intended plans turn into wishful thinking. Discipline is rarely something that simply happens in one action or in one day. Discipline is a collection of small, daily habits that form together to produce a solid foundation. This is why discipline should be instilled first. Just think about it with these examples: young children, newly assembled teams, or military boot camps. All examples demonstrate why instilling discipline at the start is key.

I believe most people can read the same word or phrase, but yet interpret it entirely differently. I have found it crucial to clearly define the keywords in your program's culture if you want your team or organization to truly live by it. When a keyword or phrase loses its intended interpretation or meaning, the effect is lost. For our basketball team, we chose to define the word discipline as, "The ability to do the same thing over and over again with no regard for your circumstance or environment." We defined this by using simple examples such as making your bed each day. Can you get up each day, and make your bed? Are you willing to do it regardless of whether you woke up late and or if you plan to get right back into your bed after class? If something as simple as this is easy for you, then you probably have had discipline instilled within you early in life. If it is more difficult for you, then recognizing that discipline is a learned habit that you can master.

Most of us believe that we are disciplined people. Actually, we all desire to be disciplined, and we know it's going to be the key to positive results. I think it's best to rate it, so you have a true picture of where your discipline level is and where it has got to be to reach your goals. First, you should pick something that is pretty simple (like making your bed) to use as the test. See how many days in a row you can go without failing. Now, the first expression of failure is going to be the thought of, "Nah, not today." Or, "I'm gonna cut the corner this one time." Honestly, to me, that's the largest failure, because you lost in your mind. But, with the activity of actually not making your bed, you cannot lie to yourself. You didn't do it, period. You'll be tested during this activity. Journal it. See if you will find that excuses are easy to make on day one or day seven. How many days in a row can you go? If this is pretty simple, then stick with that activity and add another one. Continue until you feel strong enough to say, "I am a disciplined person." As you journal, you can work each day to improve your level of discipline. Remember, it is a learned skill.

When you are living daily with a strong base of discipline, it will produce confidence in leading others.

When you are living daily with a strong base of discipline, it will produce confidence in leading others. The magic happens when each individual within the group learns to touch the lines within their level of discipline. Forget the thought of cutting corners because you know that even a small slip will ruin the habit that you have worked to create. When your entire family and organization buys into the power of discipline and sees it as a powerful word and not a word that includes punishment, then you are on the way to something special. As you work to elevate your discipline level you will need to give permission for someone to hold you accountable. There's nothing like a really good accountability partner that you trust and respect. Get a plan and get to work. Discipline is a foundation principle of future success.

MACYOLOGY:

DISCIPLINE IS THE ABILITY TO DO THE SAME THING OVER AND OVER AGAIN WITH NO REGARD FOR YOUR CIRCUMSTANCE OR ENVIRONMENT

The Story

One of the greatest stories of success I saw as a coach was the transformation of a senior shooting guard. She had always been a really good basketball player, but her daily life and fundamental habits always got in the way. She could shoot the ball like an absolute pro. God had blessed her with more ability than the average kid. However, she struggled with outside distractions and each year it would bite her one way or another. I am thankful that I got a chance to coach and watch the development of this superstar. It's one of the greatest success stories of habit changing and results I've ever seen.

I believe that as a coach, when you allow a player to underachieve and not reach their full potential then you have failed that player. As uncomfortable as it may be, you must continue to confront habits that will cause them to fail in the long run. Now, this is obviously going to cause conflict between the coach and the player. This senior shooting guard and I had more than our fair share of conflict. My consistent message became, "I am not going away." At some point, you have to be willing not to quit on a kid. They will always quit before I do. That's my promise.

I am not sure when the light switch actually went off, but it did. Oh, my goodness, did it go off! The senior had a revelation and decided it was time to be great, and she attacked. The mindset became, "Tell me what it takes, and I will do it." She narrowed her thoughts and removed distractions. The results came almost immediately. She had a microfocus like one I had never seen in a player. She stayed in the gym completing daily shooting workouts, did extra conditioning, and had a clean diet. These positive habits were seen each day, but even more importantly she removed all of her negative habits. She kicked them out the door. Her weekend distractions got replaced with a basketball.

She had a plan and she stuck to the plan. It wasn't just to shoot more. It was making 500 shots. It wasn't just drinking more water. It was drinking 100 ounces. She practically wore the coaches out asking for more training and accountability. It was a real sight of beauty. The basket all of a sudden got bigger, and her confidence grew. By the end of her senior season, she was one of the best players on the court. This was her dream come true. She shot the ball better than she ever had in her career as well as had the endurance to play extended minutes. As the coach, I was so proud of how she committed to defending. Sometimes shooters get caught up in only shooting and forget the other elements of the game. She knew her goal was to play, contribute and finish her career strong. She did that, plus more in my mind.

Now, it took extreme discipline and focus. The results she experienced will be with her for a lifetime. Typically, when you see this type of focus and results, it is that someone's A.O.F. (ass is on fire). In this case, it was the end of her career. All situations are different, but A.O.F. is what brings humans into action. This level of discipline produced incredible success. I would imagine this demonstration of consistent discipline enabled this player to be confident in other areas of her life. This is the power of discipline. When you see a goal accomplished, then it only inspires and motivates others toward this same direction. When you combine hard work with discipline there's nothing that cannot be accomplished. I know that this senior shooting guard now knows that with discipline, life feels really good.

- CHAPTER 12 -

RECOGNIZE THAT EVERYTHING IS REVIEWABLE

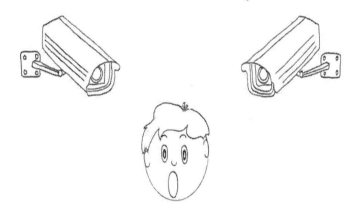

A player says, "Coach, I did not foul her! And I didn't say anything to the official." "Okay," I say as I am revving up to defend our player. I didn't see it, but the player is telling me that she didn't do it! Then I automatically say, "I've got your back." I know you've seen it a hundred times while watching games. The story plays out where the coach goes straight to the official to defend the action of the player. All of this is happening while the video is being reviewed. The video is very clear. It happened, and there are going to be consequences. The coach looks silly when defending what is very clearly an issue, but as coaches, we do it! The team and individual are now going to have a consequence. In basketball, it's two free throws and a personal foul. The game of life mirrors this same action in sports.

In corporate America, it looks more like this scenario. We get told that our emails are being reviewed. Or we get asked for our credit card statement. It will make you feel like a total criminal. I have been accused of things that I would never even dream of doing and learned that once there is an accusation, you are guilty until you prove that you are innocent. It feels dirty, it is exhausting, and it is wrong. It is the reality of the world we are living in.

You lie, you cheat, you steal. It's reviewable, and the consequences are inevitable. Now, we all realize that sometimes it's not quite as quick of a decision as a technical foul in a basketball game, but it can be just as devastating to a family, a team, and a person. If we could go into all conversations thinking that it is going to get replayed on the news at 6:00 pm or broadcasted at a church on Sunday, would we reconsider the words we use? I have often wondered why we are sometimes more caring or even more polite when we answer the phone and a telemarketer is on the other end than we are to the people in our own homes. This phone call is typically being recorded and that person's job is being assessed. What if conversations in our own home were as reviewable and accessible? Would we adjust and be more kind? I sometimes see where we are less understanding to the person that loves us under our own roof than we are to complete strangers.

I initially resisted using text messaging and having a social media account. I fought like crazy when I switched from a Blackberry to an iPhone! Now, I have learned how to use iCloud, design an email template, and order off of Amazon. We all know relationships that have started and ended due to technology. We also know of jobs that have ended or elevated because of phones. It's the world we are in and it is a scary world without built-in discipline and margin. It takes utilizing discipline and emotional intelligence in a heated moment. It takes recognizing and pausing before hitting send on the text or email. I have learned to be alert to all emails, disciplined with text messaging and to always stay wide right of anything that can be perceived as not above board. Based upon learning the hard way, I will always over-communicate what we are doing, and I open everything we

> *Live a life that you want to be reviewed and recorded.*

ever do to anyone that wants to take a look. I am sad to say that I've experienced the ugly side of college athletics, but I am proud of how we ran our program and the people we developed out of it.

My parents told me way back in the old days, not to write it down if you did not want it to be known! This was when love notes were still left in book bags and way before the ability to simply copy, paste and send to the entire world was invented. We all must build boundaries and recognize the consequences and the successes surrounding reviewable content. One major point I think is worth noting is that we cannot allow anything to cause fear in our lives. This is no way to live and fear causes misery. Live a life that you want to be reviewed and recorded. Look around at the world we live in. We either adjust quickly or end up dying by the technology.

MACYOLOGY:

THE GAME OF LIFE MIRRORS THE GAME OF BASKETBALL

The Story

I coached out of fear. Fear of losing. Fear of not being good enough. Fear of being fired. It sucks! There's nothing fun in the sport when this is how you live each day. It impacts all areas of life. Your family, your personal life, your interaction with the staff, fans, and your team. I was miserable and it made everyone around me miserable.

The result equaled losing and more losing. I am one of the most hard-headed people in the world, I think. I was convinced that with more practice, more film, and more one-on-one work we would win. We did more each and every day and we lost more and more. How does this make any sense? We were doing quality work and there were no positive results from it. I screamed and yelled at everyone. Do more and do it now. The issue was that my passion was coming from a place of fear and not from a place of assurance and contentment to help others succeed.

At this point, I was broken. I had no answers and was so angry I think I stopped searching for the answers. Then it happened. I was invited to attend a luncheon that was a game changer. I met a former high school basketball coach, turned author, that helped me see and change my heart. I immediately bought his book and it was like he was speaking directly to me. I'd lost my way and I had lost my purpose as to why I wanted to be a coach in the first place.

I sat down with my team and shared with them what I felt like was occurring within me. I saw more clearly and was sorry for the errors I had made to that point. I wish I could have watched myself on video and I could have recognized my errors more quickly. We were on a double-digit losing streak at the time. We definitely didn't start winning right away, but we started improving. Our practices were sharper, and it seemed like we all enjoyed being at practice. We played and worked harder for one another. It started to be fun again.

I went back and watched our practices. It was night and day. I re-watched the games too. They were also night and day. We even went back and clipped before and after the "heart check" adjustment to make the point. It helps me to this day remember my why, my purpose, and my heart. I coached every practice, every game and every moment for the players. When I learned that with fear life is shallow, I then made the choice to remove fear. It made us more successful and it allowed me to find my happiness in coaching again.

- CHAPTER 13 -

TAKE YOUR EYES OFF OF YOURSELF

I believe it is human nature in most situations for people to initially think, "How does this affect *me*?" I also believe we all have a selfish streak that can take over any minute in a situation. Selfishness can quickly show its ugly head when we start to ask, "Why is this happening to me?" Or when we start thinking, "Wait, what about me?" The more questions we start asking, the more selfish we become, and our eyes are totally focused on ourselves during these times.

I can tell you that nothing good happens when it's only about yourself. When your eyes are only on yourself it is a very shallow and empty way to live. When you only do it for yourself it becomes the easiest way to set yourself up for failure. It is also the easiest way to make the decision to quit something quickly. Life is not only about you. Life is about a bigger purpose. Life is about having an awesome group of people to do it with each day. Within a sports team, coaches constantly preach about the team concept which I believe to totally be right.

Use an example like the star on a sports team or the lead singer in a band. If the star player is successful and the team is winning, then they always enjoy it more. When the focus can be about the team's success versus their own stat line, life is better. When it is only about the star player's scoring average and performance, then the stress and pressure will mount quickly. It can become a weight that is impossible to carry each day. The best way I've seen it done is to make it about everyone else doing well and invest in something bigger than yourself. This does not mean that you do not experience individual success, but it does mean you do not live for it or die for it.

I have been fortunate enough to coach absolutely incredible teams and travel to cool places, but it would not have been very much fun alone. I've said it and will say it again. When you are in the picture, it's more difficult to see outside of the frame. This may cause some regrets and decisions you wish you could have adjusted. When you cannot see it clearly enough or quickly enough mistakes are made.

Trust me, my most memorable experiences in life happened when I took my eyes off of myself. When I saw the team celebrate a victory and I soaked it up simply because I was so happy that they got to experience the moment, then it felt like a success. Personally, when you can see your family shine it makes you feel their same glow.

When life becomes less about "win-win" and more about let me help you win this moment, then life gives you more than you take, and that is the victory. Wake up and love the tribe you are with on this journey but be sure to pick the right tribe to love. Remember, someone else could be in that seat at any point. Do it the best you can each day because it's not guaranteed.

> *Do it the best you can each day because it's not guaranteed.*

The Story

My first ever job out of college was a real lesson in what college coaching is all about and I learned that it is not for everyone. Either you are cut out for the demands of a coaching life or you are not. My head coach and the entire experience as an assistant coach there taught me more in one year than I could have possibly learned in five seasons. I already knew that the early bird got the worm, only the strong survive and that the show goes on with or without you. I would continue to learn much, much more that season.

It was a transformative year that built a lot of my coaching philosophies. The lessons and foundations that were established, I've never forgotten. I've been coaching for 18 years and the little voice in the back of my mind hears one sentence each and every day as I open my office door: "Heather Macy, imagine you are walking down the street and a Mack Truck goes off of the road and hits you. If you cannot make it into work tomorrow, then there will be someone ready to step right in and take your place." I would think, "Okay coach, you are nuts, but I understand." Then he would remind me, "Never, ever have an overexaggerated sense of self-importance."

I can hear my head coach saying it and reminding me right now, "Mack Truck Principle, Mace." As harsh as it may have seemed at the time, I learned it is true. It kept me motivated to be better each day. I learned that not only are people waiting in line to replace you at your job, but there are hundreds hoping you get hit by the Mack Truck. Many are mostly concerned with who's going to get an interview for your job. Your current job is sometimes seen as an opportunity by most people to sit in your office chair. Trust me, most think they are capable of doing your job and that they can actually do your job way better than you do it. This actually has always allowed me to stay humble. I was reminded daily of this fact that season and it helped me be better, quicker. I would always remind myself that I am not the only person in the world that can take on this job, and someone is definitely out there that can do it better than I can.

This story has become my reminder to approach each day with urgency. It also allowed me to invest in others instead of only myself each day. Could I leave each program better than I found it? Could I help other people accomplish their goals? The goal has always been to value the opportunity I'd been given and to do my best each and every day with it. If and when someone else steps into *your job* and does it better than you, tip your hat and move forward.

- CHAPTER 14 -
REPEATABILITY

I said what? That's not what I meant or thought I said, exactly. Wait, when did I say it? To whom? Things that barely hit my memory are now stories that others are telling and retelling and sometimes making decisions on it. I just don't get it. A person's title can totally change someone's credibility. It really makes very little sense. I'm still the same person with the same opinions and skill sets as

I was a day ago, but now I have a new title. So, here's some solid advice, that I wish I knew before the mistake: understand that as your title or position changes, so does the perception of your opinion or words.

So, recognizing that your repeatability will change prior to your promotion is key. I realized it the hard way. When someone asked me a question or for my opinion, I'd always just share. Yes, sometimes this is a bad idea. If what I am about to share is now going to be a new truth to someone, it is vital to acknowledge this fact. A lot of feelings could get hurt and a lot of information can get repeated incorrectly.

A good friend told me this analogy and I've learned that it is so true. Imagine your relationship with that person is like a yardstick or a long-handled spoon. When the spoon is being placed into boiling water, it mirrors the testing of our relationships. When you first stick that long-handled spoon into the boiling water you put in just a little to be sure you don't get burned. When you aren't burned, you can go a little deeper into the boiling water. Then, you allow the spoon in a little more. We do the same thing with relationships. We share a little at first. When we see that we can trust that person, we can share a little more.

However, once you are burned and the information is shared and repeated that now must become the depth of that relationship. It is powerful to learn how deep a relationship can actually go.

When you have a friend and choose to share something privately, you are taking a risk that the share will eventually not stay between just the two of you. That big share or vulnerability that you believe is in confidence may or may not be. If that information stays between you both, then you will feel safer to share

> *Always recognize that when you are in someone's circle, value it, respect it, and see it as the ultimate responsibility.*

again. Now you keep going until your boundary gets established based upon trust. Once the information gets repeated then the boundary needs to be firmly set at that point. Trust me, everything will get repeated eventually.

This is a pretty powerful analogy if you will pay attention and set the boundaries in your life. It's worth noting that it does not mean that once a person breaks your trust or over shares your conversations, then you are unable to be friends. It simply means that your relationship and trust with this person can only go to a certain point. It allows you to create clear boundaries with the people in your life.

What a great way to assess your friends, acquaintances, and partners. This is an especially important activity when you are selecting who is in your inner circle. In my experience, there are only a few that can be in that circle. And even less that will still be in that circle when the water really starts to boil. Always recognize that when you are in someone's circle, value it, respect it, and see it as the ultimate responsibility.

MACYOLOGY:

RECOGNIZING THE LONG-HANDLED SPOON RELATIONSHIP

The Story

So, I am simply sitting and watching a basketball game. It's no big deal and all kinds of people stop over and speak. Some sit and small talk, some sit and need a favor, and some sit for an objective. On this particular day, I did not recognize that my words had any repeatability. As a matter of fact, I did not even know the concept at all. This is when I learned my lesson.

I was simply asked, "What do you think about Sally's game, coach?" My quick response was, "She hasn't gotten much better over the last year or so." Now, for me this did not mean she's a terrible player, or that I don't like her game, or that she is not good enough to play in our program. However, I might as well have said exactly all of those things that day. As quickly as I said this statement, my input got repeated equally as quick. It made it all the way back to the player's family and the coach. We then got removed from her recruiting list because she thought we said she was not good enough. Now, this was a player that I did actually think was good enough and a player that I thought we could really help with maximizing her potential. Yikes! What had I done? We lost a really good player that could have helped us win, simply because I answered wrong. Maybe not wrong, but too direct for the environment or, as I learned, too direct for my title.

This really made me pause and think. And it truly made me learn to always pause before giving an answer. Repeatability can ruin a relationship the same way it can inflate someone's reputation. If I was asked what kind of coach someone may be, I then had another decision to make. I could say that this coach is the best or worst recruiter I'd ever worked with. I could also build another coach's reputation as the best X's and O's coach out there or someone simply not very good with game-time decisions. It's interesting, isn't it? We all have a choice to make and it is a powerful one. Choose wisely because you are impacting lives with your opinions. They have repeatability.

We are all people. We are not our titles. We do, however, have a responsibility once we have accepted a title. I really wish someone could have explained that to me early on in my career. I have always looked at myself in the mirror as just Heather. A kid from Hamptonville, NC that is willing to work her tail off to get what she wants. It was hard to adjust when all of a sudden, "Heather" became recognizable with some new level of normal. I had a lot of friends and a lot of social obligations. I do mostly believe it was because they really liked Heather, and maybe they did. I had no boundaries in any relationships. I joked, played around, and was loose with my words. With experience, I have learned, grown, and become stronger from being left in the hot boiling water. Thanks so much. I got it this time!

- CHAPTER 15 -

COMPETE ALWAYS IN ALL WAYS

O kay, women, I am talking directly to you. I absolutely believe that there can be two powerful women in the same organization. Actually, there can be two women who are ultra-successful in that company at the same time. Women can also help one another to be amazing. Listen closely: there can even be two women in high-level leadership positions. We all know that two is only better than one if two act as one. In any team or organization, we must all act as one if we want to reach the goals quickly and efficiently. Ladies, the men have it down and mastered. They understand that when one man gets the promotion, then he will be able to promote the next man up later on. Why can't we, as women, see this same formula? It is absolutely genius, and we should follow suit and duplicate this process. We should all understand that women can help other women by being the best version of themselves each and every day to help each other elevate our game and organization. If you do the same for one another, then, in the end, we will be amazing, and our organization will thrive.

One major theme of all successful teams and organizations is that they compete each day. When we are able to compete each day, we can all elevate and get what we want out of life. We are all sitting way over there at this very moment, and the goals in life we want to accomplish are sitting way over the hill in the far distance. How are we getting there and how are we getting there together in the fastest and most efficient way possible? Well, let's straighten the string. As a reminder, *MINDSET LESSON #1* says in part, "Issues and dramas are simply distractions." Recognizing and adjusting along the way will determine how quickly you are able to "straighten the string" directly to your goal.

You see, everyone in our camp and specifically in your tribe must believe in this concept; otherwise, it takes much longer to get to the goal. Each time an obstacle happens, it will loop our string wider, and the people we choose to associate with will determine how quickly we can straighten it back. Each time we have internal resistance, our string loops even wider. The longer it takes to get back on track, the farther we get from our goal. I've coached teams where both exist, and the key is that everyone in our locker room is pulling together. Everyone needs to pull in the same direction. Compete each day but remember that the competition must stay outside of your home and locker room.

We will accomplish more and much faster when we compete together in the environment in which we work. Competing isn't a reaction at the end of a quarter, the end of a contract, or the end of a season. "To compete" should be the way we show up each day. Living in an offensive posture and on the attack should be the norm. We can be competitive each day inside the same organization without feeling like the person in the office beside of us is the competition. Easily defined: competitive is striving together; competition is striving against. Let me clarify this point once again; competing is striving together while competition is striving against someone.

> *. . . competitive is striving together; competition is striving against.*

The key is aligning our group, team, and family is to realize we can make each other better each day by competing. The competition in this world is already tough enough, so recognizing the difference is paramount. The loop in our string gets wider when we are treating our teammates as the competition. Wake up and strive together by competing within your tribe.

MACYOLOGY:

DEFINE COMPETITIVE VS. COMPETITION

The Story

"Compete! Raise your competitive index. Everyone must go fight hard for what they want." This was my mindset for a long time: eat or be eaten. Well, I had to learn the hard way that this is not the way to mesh a team or group of people together for one common goal. The key is getting us all to compete and to understand that the competition includes the external variables. As we get ready to play a basketball game, the competition lies in the different colored uniform and not between the people inside your own locker room.

This is the key, but the sad truth is that it doesn't always work this way. When the locker room becomes invaded by the competitor, then the result will always be negative even when the scoreboard is in your favor.

We had a season where I know for sure we had players that were competitors, and I mean literally competitors. They wanted to win out in everything: in every drill, in every team building game, and even in academic accolades. At first, I thought, "YES, exactly what I have always wanted to coach." Then as the team started to storm and form, I realized this mentality extended to who was playing more minutes, who was taking more shots, and who was scoring more points. Oh no! We were not competing with one another as I thought; instead, we were actually competing against one another. There wasn't a game all season where I thought the other team beat us. I thought each game we lost was actually because we pulled against one another.

In many games, I would look down the bench and see mad faces because of the amount of playing time they got or because someone else was having their best game, I realized the distinction between the words had to be defined. Once I was able to define the two words: competitive vs. competition, then it made what we were looking for much clearer for the team. I believe that had each player understood and lived the distinction between the two words, then each player could have realized that truly without the other person we weren't going to experience as much individual or team success. The magic can only happen after that point is clearly defined and lived.

I don't know that during that specific season the words were clarified enough or that they were actually ever truly realized. I do know that at the end of it all, we knew we could have done more, but we could never have done more alone. I am still thankful for that lesson. Surrounding yourself with competitive people is awesome, but only if those competitors are willing to take their eyes off themselves and compete to elevate the team. I am now able to still recruit competitive people, but better direct them from the start into utilizing this trait for positive gains.

MY EQ JOURNEY

It's a fact: I do care about winning a great deal, but I also care about the people a whole lot more. The gap was between my truth and their truth. For me, the key was demonstrating this fact consistently and clearly to the people I love the most. I learned that my major mistake was the inability to understand how others may feel and to deeply empathize with their emotions while also being aware of my emotions and the scope of the environment.

The term "emotional intelligence" was a foreign one to me. I first stumbled onto the term while reading a book by a former collegiate coach. She was a very successful college coach whom I respected very much. I was hoping to learn how she transitioned so strongly from college coaching into corporate coaching. She utilized a chapter on EQ in her book to describe how this one skill was vital to her success. I immediately started researching and learning more about EQ. I purchased a quick read to learn more and this is when my defining moment around emotional intelligence happened. At the end of this book, it offered a four-part quiz on EQ. I made a 70 on all but one part of the quiz. Well, that is all I needed: a challenge. I obviously am not accustomed to failing a quiz and when I did, I wanted to attack the weakness right away. This is when my EQ journey officially began.

I was reading, asking, and stumbling upon all and everything EQ. The more I learned, the more my interest was sparked. The law of attraction elevated quickly during this journey. EQ started popping up everywhere. I watched TED Talks, YouTube videos and read more and more. Conversations would start to lean toward and around the topic. After being educated on the fact that this skill could grow, I was totally up for it. I was shocked to learn that this is a learned skill where unlike IQ you can grow 7-10% with proper training. I knew there was something beyond what I was doing each day with my team and me personally. There was more out there to help a team be elite. I just did not know what it was, but my gut said there was more, and I was in a search to find it. I believe I found it with my study of emotional intelligence.

In 2017, I was introduced to Dr. Izzy Justice. He offered a certification in Emotional Intelligence (EQ). This experience was game-changing. He related EQ to me through neuroscience and performance strategy, and I was sold. It allowed me to learn and explore my emotions. Once I was able to master recognizing my own emotions, it became evident how I could better express and relate to others' emotions more effectively. I went on a year-long journey of exploring how these techniques fit into my life. Practicing mindfulness and awareness of my five senses became a daily practice in my life. I knew that before I could implement these techniques within our team, I would need to not only buy in but to live it.

After seeing how this practice elevated my life, I was committed to integrating it into our team. I first asked the team if they knew what percentage the game of basketball is mental to physical. I got all kinds of responses back from the team between 50/50 to 90/10. We decided that within our program it is 70/30. If we truly believed this and knew it to be true, then we must train it. We gradually started utilizing the techniques and practices daily to elevate the mental side of performance. As we progressed, we added more and more. Eventually, our team learned how to be elite and prepare for the highest level of performance. We developed a language that we all used within our program to discuss our emotions and gave one another permission to help hold one another accountable. The language allowed us to talk about our emotions in a simple way, when it can sometimes be the most complex of conversations. We also learned to plan for mishaps and how to remove fear from the game.

Learning EQ techniques has allowed me to not only care at an elite level but express that I care. This has become important to me that the people I love and cherish the most actually know that I care. It has also allowed me to help more people. When I share the details of my EQ journey with other coaches and teams, I know right away that I am able to change people's lives.

I believe that influencing and impacting is the greatest win in life. After all, life is not a sequence of events. It is an opportunity that we only have one time. I figure the best way to maximize it is to keep your eyes off of yourself. The best way to live it is to figure out a way to help other people. The goal in life is simple to me: *find a way, choose happy!*

Ask me about living life *GREEN*. Stay GREEN, my friends.

TRIBUTES

**THESE 18 TRIBUTES OF FORMER ASSISTANT
COACHES AND PLAYERS REPRESENT THE
AUTHOR'S 18 YEARS OF COLLEGE COACHING**

I n the spring of 2007, I interviewed for an assistant coaching position at Francis Marion University. That was the first day I met Heather Macy, and I knew right away that she was a special leader. Her strong belief in her coaching philosophy and her vision were apparent. I wanted to learn from her and be a part of her legacy. I was lucky and grateful to have joined her staff that year.

I have always had a strong work ethic, but Heather pushed me harder than anyone has ever pushed me. Today, I am a better person for being pushed and challenged. From day one on her staff, I truly discovered the definition of hard work. I was completely overwhelmed at first, but I came to realize that every minute detail that went into my day was an important part of Heather's program. I realized that the small things do matter. Nothing in Heather's program was ever overlooked. From always having tucked in shirts, to no earphones outside of the bus, to the locker room color schemes and decorations, Heather thought about it all.

These details, of course, carried over onto the court. Heather is extremely sharp and precise, and she had to be in order to teach the Princeton offense to a roster usually full of first-year transfers. When everyone realizes that the little things matter both on and off the court, it shows discipline. The players really need a strong sense of discipline in order to succeed both on and off the court. We would always "put our best foot forward" in everything we did. And Heather was a master at relaying that message to the girls. We knew we would always have to be disciplined in such a structured offense. But it was amazing to see how easily the girls learned because Heather pushed them just as hard as she pushed me to succeed. However, she would push each player in a different way. She would always go to great lengths to be a players' coach and really knew how to communicate with her players (especially the point guards). I remember the staff and team taking a personality assessment to see how best to approach, communicate, encourage, and motivate each other. It was really interesting and extremely helpful in communicating with the players and gaining an understanding that some girls need to be corrected immediately, while others needed a gentle reminder. Some even needed to talk about it the next day in the office. Building relationships with the players took time. As busy as Heather's schedule may have been, her door was always open to her players. She spent quality time getting to know her players on the bus, in the office, at community events: truly anywhere. All of her players respected that relationship and I believe it is the reason why we succeeded under pressure. We all trusted everything that Coach Macy said as she would reveal the game plan or draw up a game-winning play with conviction. The players would look into Coach Macy's eyes, trust what she was saying and were able to execute under pressure.

My favorite moments were always the end of practice huddles the day before a game. We would gather around half court and link arms. Heather could always command the room. Even though the girls were tired and sweaty, they were able to focus and hang on her every inspirational word. Heather talked about the "thought of the day" (TOTD) and inspired the girls to be their best, reminding them that every waking moment was an opportunity, and we needed to seize it. We knew we were always better prepared than our opponents and all we needed to do was execute our game plan. And then, playfully, Coach Macy would grab a ball and attempt to hit a half-court shot. We couldn't end practice until someone made one. It made everyone loose, happy and excited for the opportunity to win the following day. The inspiration and the impact she had on her players was always amazing to see.

I think that I have learned many lessons from Coach Heather Macy that I use in my everyday life as a wife and a mother. She has taught me to be prepared for anything, to show patience and integrity and to be a strong female leader. I value all the relationships I have built and work to maintain. One of the most important things I learned is that *success is a choice.* We choose to work hard and prepare in order to succeed. "There is no microwave to success" is one of Coach Macy's best lines. I am grateful for my experience working for Heather, and I am happy to call her my friend.

Carol Sciaretta
FMU & ECU Coach

When I think about the qualities that make a great coach, I think of Heather Macy; the connection that she has with her players, the extra hours she spends beyond a "normal" working day, and the time she put into relationships with each individual to get them to reach their potential for themselves and for the team. Coaching is not just a job for Heather, but instead a passion. As her assistant coach for three years, I saw the personal drive that she had to bring out the best in her players and the many hours she spent strategizing on how to do that. I also think about the inspiring pre-and post-games talks, intense time-outs during games, and team huddles at practice. She made me believe that our team was capable of always winning and that only the best was acceptable in all situations. Her passion and drive left a mark on many players and people that she has encountered, including me, as well as the game of basketball and the universities where she has coached.

Jami Cornwell
Pfeiffer & FMU Coach

There are numerous things I learned and have carried on with me from my time working with Coach Macy. First and foremost, I gained a better understanding of what it means to be a "player's coach." Coach Macy is definitely a coach that players want to play for and demonstrate a loyalty back to her. She puts the players and their needs ahead of anything else in her schedule. She makes time for them even when a busy schedule would be a perfect excuse to do other things.

Coach Macy also taught me the importance of preparing for March instead of November. Her method of training and not over-training is crucial for making runs late in the season. Her focus is to be ready in the most important part of the season when the games count the most. She trains the players to be ready mentally and physically to win championships. She knows her coaching philosophies (offenses and defenses) like the back of her hand and sticks to it. Coach Macy has a terrific basketball mind and passes that on to her team.

Lastly, Coach Macy has a clear vision and passion for what she wants to accomplish. Lots of people have a vision, but she has the vital ability to impart her vision to all those around her. She creates an energy that is contagious within the team and community. She makes a tremendous effort to include everyone in that vision. She works tirelessly to spread the vision of her program to anyone who wants to get 2FTN.

Ann Hancock
ECU Coach

Coach Macy's influence on my life dates all the way back to my years as a misunderstood high school kid. She impacted my life then and continues to today. Coach Macy has taught me so many lessons regarding the X's and O's of the game, but the most influential words I have taken from her had less to do with basketball strategy and more to do with succeeding in life. Exceeding expectations in all you do, going the extra mile for people and living "Two Feet In" are just a few of the many lessons I learned from Coach Macy.

I was given an opportunity to step into a new role under Coach Macy at East Carolina University and found myself in one of the most gratifying experiences of my life. I was in the presence of one of the most influential leaders in women's college basketball on a day to day basis. I was consistently challenged in many areas of my life to be the best version of myself. My experience working for Coach Macy was one that I will take with me wherever I go. She is passionate about people and bringing out the elite performer in anyone who crosses her path. Whether you are a player, staff member, fan, or someone looking for a sense of direction – you will always be on the same team. It's a team willing to go the extra mile in order to influence people and leave a lasting impact on the world.

Brittany Christian
FMU Player & ECU Coach

To have played for Coach Heather Macy was an honor and a blessing. Coach Macy gave me what I called a "second chance." Transferring to Francis Marion University from Georgia State University, I came in to play for Coach Macy my junior and senior years of college. I remember my junior year trying to find my way in a new system, and I was struggling. Coach Macy was always the type to figure out how to push every player to be their best. Whether it was long talks in the office, handwritten notes waiting for you in your mailbox, or showing you exactly what she expected and leading by example, she was always there to help. At Francis Marion, I was known as a shooter and would get very upset with myself for missing shots. I remember the day Coach told me, "Shoot every shot like it's your first one." It was the way Coach said it and how much she showed me she believed in me that made me want to be a better player. Her faith in me made me want to tattoo that same saying on my arm, and I did!

One thing that stood out to me was the fact that we would come to practice every day with a new "Thought of the Day" on the practice plan. I loved the fact that every teammate and staff member knew each TOTD and in return, it helped us as players to think about life and basketball. It motivated us to be better each day. Coach Macy always encouraged us to think and see the bigger picture. She created a family environment and that's exactly what we were, family. I appreciate all of the lessons and all of the hard work Coach Macy put in to make us successful.

Eight years later, I got a chance to be under Coach Macy's supervision once again, but this time as a part of her staff. Blessed with an opportunity to work with one of the greatest coaches in the world, I felt honored to be included as part of her staff. What better way to learn than from a leader who is loyal, has your best interest at heart, and holds you accountable? She is willing to teach you everything you need to know to be successful in this career. She has a tremendous work ethic and high-volume energy. I appreciate everything she taught me; all the conversations, the examples, the opportunities, and all the knowledge.

As Coach Macy would say, "If you stay ready, you don't have to get ready!" Coach Macy will forever be family and I'll love her always.

Eboni Fields
FMU Player & ECU Coach

Have you ever met someone unrelated to you who has impacted your life in the most positive way possible? I'm talking about truly making a difference in your life for the long haul. Whether it be by teaching you a lesson that sticks with you for life or providing you the deepest insight into situations you otherwise would not have known, Heather Macy was and is that person to me. Along with being my head coach and former boss, Heather provided what I like to call "Life Guidance" throughout our times together. She continuously challenged us to change our way of thinking. From negative to positive, from broad focus to narrow focus, from mistakes to lessons; there was always a way to put a positive spin on life.

One tool, in particular, we all became particularly fond of is the "Thought of the Day" (TOTD). Every day while I was playing and working for Heather, she would post a Thought of the Day in the locker room. From famous quotes to inspirational sayings, the TOTD was supposed to make us think, question, and reflect. One of my favorite TOTD's was a quote from a book we were reading as a team at the time: "If what you did yesterday still looks big to you, then you haven't done enough today." - Mike Krzyzewski. I specifically remember this being a TOTD after a big win in the middle of the season. It was, of course, meant to humble us, but also to remind us to stay "hungry" for the next victory.

While my on-court victories have now changed to office accomplishments, the sentiment is still there. A true competitor's nature doesn't change just because the arena has changed. This is another "Macyism" that I find myself coming back to often. The amount of time Heather invested in finding quotes and selectively choosing the situations for which it was suited to maximize the impact is just a small part of the way Coach Macy's TOTD changed the way her teams thought on and off the court, but also in life after basketball.

Danelle Downs
FMU Player & ECU Coach

As a former player of Coach Macy's, I can say she has to be one of the most passionate people I know. She instills in her players that we as women are to be aggressive and unapologetic about it. We are to go after what we want in the world. Coach Macy teaches more than just basketball; she teaches life lessons that will carry over into the lives of those she comes into contact with. She has paved the way for women to be in top positions and show that we belong. Coach Macy impacts and influences others not only through her words but in her actions as well. She continually seeks to better herself and encourages others around her to do the same.

Current College Basketball Player

My experience playing under Coach Macy was great! Having back to back to back 20 plus win seasons was an amazing feeling and a big accomplishment for us all. We went from having workouts in Christenbury Memorial Gym all summer long, to having a tough "Price of Admission" workout that built mentality. Both of these were pretty tough if you ask me, but in the end, you could see all of that hard work paying off. I learned so much throughout the 3 years spent at ECU which I still carry with me to this day. Coach Macy has taught me life lessons that I can't even imagine any other coach taking the time out to do for their players.

While at ECU we had these "Thoughts of the Day" inspirational quotes every day before heading into practice. They were so beneficial to me, because I know some days walking in for practice my head wasn't in the right place, or I would be having a bad day and reading those quotes gave me a clear mind. It also steered my focus on the greater good of my well-being. However, one of the main phrases that stuck out to me the most during our huddles and sit-downs was having a "killer mentality" on the basketball court. To me, that meant having the utmost confidence that nobody can guard me, and that I am unstoppable. Even playing professionally overseas, I still have that same mentality, because I refuse to be sent home just to have someone replace me that's not even as good as me.

Coach Macy has helped a lot of her players, and I am proud to say that she is and always will be my Coach and family. Coach, I just want to say, thank you for always believing in me even when some days I didn't believe in myself. I wouldn't be where I am at today if it weren't for the help and life lessons you've instilled in me to not just get through each day but to own each day. For that, I am forever grateful.

Abria Trice
ECU Player

When I think of Coach Macy, a few words come to mind: Winning, Leadership, Discipline, Impact, and Influence, and let's not forget, "Two Feet In."

I have been lucky to not only know her as a player but also as an employee. Coach Macy has this passion like none other. A passion for winning on the court of course, but also in life. Every day that I spent with Coach Macy included a life lesson that she made sure to tie into the game of basketball. Because of Coach Macy, I began to read more personal development books: John Maxwell books, to be exact. She taught me about life in general and how to be a great leader outside of basketball. The impact and influence she made in the earlier years as my coach definitely carried over to the woman I am now. She's intentional, resourceful, and strategic! She's always "Two Feet In" and will have your back, no matter what!

Congrats on your book, Coach Macy. It's time the world got to know and learn from such an intentional, amazing, phenom!

Simone Trice
FMU Player & ECU Coach

I played for Coach Macy at Francis Marion University from 2008-2010. Even though it was for only 2 seasons, I have lessons from her that I will carry with me for the rest of my life. During my senior year, we had a game at The OrthoCarolina Tournament vs Wingate University. It was a game that we definitely should have won easily, in my opinion, but unfortunately, we lost in the final moments after a back and forth game.

She instilled in us that losing was unacceptable and not a trait of our team, nor our program. We all took it very hard, and we were disappointed in ourselves. We headed back to the FMU campus or so we all thought. We ended up at Coach Macy's house instead of the campus, and we were all confused. The entire team and coaching staff went inside and sat on the couch and floor wondering what was next. It seems funny now, but boy were we scared at the time.

Instead of yelling at us or lecturing us, she expressed her disappointment in us calmly and we engaged in a round table discussion in her living room. She let us express how we all felt and express ideas about things that we thought we need to change as a team, so a game like that doesn't happen again. I gained a new level of respect for her after that night and not just as a coach, but as a person. It's easy to yell in anger and to criticize us after a deflating loss, but she chose a different route and wanted to know how we felt. I absolutely respect that more than anything. I personally think that made her a better coach: she's the best.

Dawn Coleman
FMU Player

I am grateful to have played under Coach Macy for the majority of my collegiate career. Initially, I knew that I was signing up to play under a proven head coach. However, what I didn't know was that I was also gaining an influencer that had mastered the art of motivation and self-discipline. Our back-to-back 20+ regular season wins and postseason appearances were a testament to the culture of discipline, hard work, and positivity that Coach Macy created early on within our team. A large source of motivation for me came through her daily lessons and TOTD's (thought of the day). It helped build my mentality and ultimately shaped me into one of the best players in my school's history.

Throughout my career, I faced many adverse situations, both on and off the court. One of the biggest lessons I learned came from a TOTD. The thought was, "Don't break before the breakthrough." I was at a point in which I was about to break both physically and mentally, and this simple, yet powerful message carried me through those tough times. There were many lessons like this one that helped mold me into the person that I am today.

I am proud to have played for Coach Macy and would encourage everyone to try to apply these lessons to their everyday lives.

Jada Payne
ECU Player

Coach Macy's leadership style was one that motivated, inspired, and energized me as an athlete. It provided me with a sense of achievement, belonging, recognition, and self-esteem that allowed me to feel in control over my life. She enriched my ability to live up to my own ideas and expectations.

Life is part of the game of basketball. Coach was able to utilize a variety of physical conditioning that was appropriate to prevent the team from injuries and also build mental toughness. Coach provided both growth and developmental skills which guided me to be ready for competition. Her teaching and communication styles were effective in teaching the fundamentals of the game while identifying my weakness and maximizing my potential.

Thank you, coach! You helped me to get the most out of every practice and every single game that I played under your leadership.

Dominique China
Pfeiffer Player

A famous coach once said, "Motivation is the extra push needed to reach a goal. One of the best ways to motivate is to be sure that you have surrounded yourself with great teammates. Once you come to know and understand the people on your team as individuals, you will come to realize that everyone needs to be motivated differently." Coach Macy is the type of coach and leader who always finds a new way to motivate and push players individually and come together as a team. On the court, she possesses a contagious fire and tenacity to fight for 40 minutes. Off the court, her door is always open to talk and get to know you better or watch the film to elevate your game. She never asked more from the team or an individual than she was willing to give herself. I know that this book will deliver the same.

Dominique Powell
FMU Player

I was always taught by my parents that you have to work hard to get what you want out of life. I've always remembered that fact in life and it has played a major part of who I am. Coach Macy taught me that and, more importantly, how to be comfortable with being uncomfortable. She always challenged me as a player and then as a coach for the time that I was able to coach alongside her.

As a player, I remember her challenging me to be a vocal leader. I always was the person that led by example, so it was hard for me in the beginning. But Coach Macy challenged me to be vocal, and my teammates made that job easier for me. After all the work Coach Macy put in with me, I became not only a leader by example but a vocal leader as well. She did not only challenge me on the court but also in my coaching career. I've learned so much in the amount of time I worked with her and I am thankful for it. I will continue to carry with me the idea of being comfortable with being uncomfortable. She isn't only a coach, but a person that stays in contact, wanting to know what is going on in your life, and how your family is doing. It is more than just basketball with her. Thank you, Coach.

Celeste Stewart
ECU Coach & Player

Being chosen to be a part of Coach Macy's family at East Carolina seemed so natural to me that I only took 1 of my 5 visits my sophomore year at Jones Junior College. After seeing how much she actually cared for her players, it made me want to play for her and I signed early. She possesses qualities in a coach that reminded me of the values which were instilled in me as a child. To me, her motto "Two Feet In" represented hard work, perseverance, and servitude. Hard work encompassed dedication to not only learning the game of basketball but also the game of life. Perseverance was necessary to sustain the great responsibility of being a winner for people in order to motivate and succeed. As for servitude, God's law was the focus. It became the art of "doing unto others as you would have them to do unto you." This inspired me to become my best self and I sincerely thank Coach Macy for the opportunity.

Current College Basketball Player

Coach Heather Macy is passionate, charismatic, and competitive above all other things. Coach Macy exudes strength and leadership qualities that make you want to go run through a brick wall for her. Before playing for Coach Macy, I had played at a previous school and had 1 year of eligibility left. My goal was to finish my collegiate basketball career on a positive note.

Under Coach Macy, I flourished. Her belief and confidence in me on a daily basis both on the court and off made all the difference. Coach Macy provided me with daily life examples and lessons. For instance, one TOTD that I still think about often is: Live your dash. The meaning was about how your life is made up of two dates, and the dash in between is how you choose to live. Coach Macy was challenging us and empowering us to get the most out of our dash of time.

Lastly, my experience as a player under Coach Macy renewed my love for the game. The lessons learned during my time with Coach Macy are implemented constantly in my life today. I am beyond grateful to have been coached and mentored by such a powerful leader as Coach Heather Macy.

Kristen Gaffney
ECU Player

I only got to experience Coach Macy as my Coach for a short period of time, but she's someone I plan on keeping in my life forever. Starting from the very beginning, getting to know coach through the recruiting process, I knew she was different from most coaches I'd met. From just the first few conversations, she told me how much she believed in me as a potential player in her program and as an athlete in general. As a result, committing to Coach Macy was one of the most confident decisions I'd ever made in my life, and I was excited to play for someone who truly made me feel the most wanted.

Upon coming to play for Coach Macy, I knew that being 20 hours from home was going to be a challenge but knowing how much she believed in me is what made me feel like I could handle it. She was always hard on me, she was hard on all of us, but the difference between her and other coaches I've had was that while she was being hard on you, she was teaching you how to deal with it. She taught us how to be mentally tough and not let anyone else but you control your emotions. There were 3 ideas that always stood out to me the most. She encouraged the team to buy into these 3 ideas, and I don't think I'll ever forget them.

1. You are the chief interpreter of your own reality.
2. Elite performers leave nothing to chance, ever.
3. Drama, negativity, and issues are just distractions from your goals.

I noticed that when I started to truly understand the quotes or themes she was preaching and not just remembering the words to be sure I wasn't making us run, it was easier for me to understand Coach Macy, what she wanted for me, and what she wanted for the program as a whole. I had bought in even if I wasn't sure what the future would hold. Finding out I wouldn't get the chance to play for her for the next four years was heartbreaking. In those few short months, I was already improving as a player and a person thanks to her. I am forever grateful I got to be in her presence as much as I did and I wouldn't change a thing. Coach Macy helped me believe in myself, and if she had that great an impact on my life in just a few short months I know she is going to continue to make an impact on people's lives in everything she chooses to do. She is truly one of a kind and will forever be a blessing to my family and me. Love you always Coach!

Current College Basketball Player

I played for Coach Macy as a junior at Pfeiffer University. She transformed the basketball program there and was able to lead us to the NCAA tournament. Coach Macy put in incredible amounts of hard work and dedication. She poured herself into the women's basketball team each day. I was a well-rounded player, but coach Macy helped me see the potential in my game that had not yet been unlocked. She not only helped me develop my basketball skills, but she also taught me what it meant to be a leader on more than the score sheet while being a part of a very talented team. It was through her leadership and knowledge of basketball that led the Pfeiffer Falcons to victories and one of the most successful seasons ever at the school. I will always remember Coach Macy for her coaching skills, but more importantly for her dedication and leadership.

Kalee Smith
Pfeiffer Player

ABOUT THE AUTHOR

Heather Macy, the all-time winningest coach in the history of East Carolina University women's basketball, is the definition of passion and focus. She is not only a coach, but an author, motivator, and leader. Macy prides herself in helping others reach their goals. Her philosophy of impacting and influencing is based upon building confidence, instilling discipline and keeping the intent based upon, YOU winning.

Macy owns a career record of 248-155 including a 134-117 overall mark during her tenure at ECU. During the 2014-15 campaign, she became the first coach in program history to lead the Pirates to 20 or more wins in three-straight seasons. A 22-11 overall record and a third consecutive Women's National Invitation Tournament (WNIT) appearance capped off the three most successful seasons ever in program history. Her fifth season at ECU was historic in a number of ways as she earned her 200th-career win, ECU broke the school record for blocks (181), posted the second most steals (380) and second best three-point percentage (.355), while forcing the third most turnovers (714) in a season in program history. The Pirates also defeated their first ranked opponent since 2007. During this a, ECU's only WNBA trainee was selected by the Washington Mystics.

Jada Payne, was one of six players selected to the All-American Athletic Conference First Team, while junior I'Tiana Taylor was named to the second team in addition to being chosen as the American Conference's Newcomer-of-the Year. Payne also broke a pair of her own single-season school records, netting 80 three-pointers to best her previous year's total by 10, while making 86.5 percent of her free throws to top her 86.5 percent clip.

The 2012-13 ECU concluded the season with an impressive 14-1 record inside Minges Coliseum as they set a new program record for the most home wins in a single season. Included in that mark was a school-record 26-game home winning streak that began one year prior, and at one point, stood as the second-longest among NCAA Division I teams. At the conclusion of the season, Macy was named Conference-USA Coach of the Year, while junior forward Kristine Mial garnered C-USA Sixth Player of the Year accolades, and senior point guard Celeste Stewart was selected to the C-USA All-First Team while redshirt senior center Britny Edwards collected C-USA All-Defensive Team honors. In addition to the stellar year the Pirates had on the court, Macy's squad also excelled in the classroom. Thirteen team members from the 2012-13 squad earned Conference-

USA Honor Roll status. Her team also had the highest team GPA for all C-USA teams for the second consecutive year.

Macy previously led Francis Marion University for three seasons, averaging 25 wins per season. In 2009-2010 the team went 27-5 and subsequently earned a berth to the NCAA Division II Tournament and advanced to the second round. Additionally, FMU led the nation in steals per game for the third straight year. They also ranked second in both scoring offense and assists while earning a No. 20 national ranking in the final USA Today/ESPN Division II Top 25 poll. During the '08-09 campaign, Macy directed the Patriots to a 27-5 record, a No. 14 national ranking, a second-straight Peach Belt Conference regular-season championship and advanced to the Sweet Sixteen. It marked the third time in as many seasons that a Macy-coached team led the nation in scoring offense. She also earned Peach Belt Conference Coach of the Year honors for a third-straight campaign. In her first season at the helm of the program, Macy guided FMU to a 21-9 mark and was named Peach Belt Coach of the Year. After inheriting a squad that was 6-22 the season before her arrival, the 21 wins equaled the largest turn-around in NCAA Division II that year and the eighth-best in history. FMU captured a share of the Peach Belt Conference regular-season title and earned a bid to the NCAA Division II Tournament.

The Hamptonville, N.C., native arrived at FMU after serving two seasons as head coach at Pfeiffer University. In 2006-07, she took the Falcons to a 26-5 record, the Carolina-Virginia Athletics Conference (CVAC) regular-season and tournament championships, and an appearance in the NCAA Division II Tournament. The team's record represented the fourth-best turnaround in Division II that campaign. She was named the C-VAC Coach of the Year and Pfeiffer led the nation in scoring offense.

Heather is a highly requested speaker at Fortune 500 companies, civic and non-profit organizations, hospitals, schools, camps, and clinics. During these presentations, topics like teamwork, accountability, discipline, and emotional intelligence are explored. Heather graduated cum laude in Sport and Exercise Studies from Greensboro College in 2000, where she played basketball and tennis. She ended her career 11th on the Pride's career scoring list and in the top 10 for assists. In 2002, she earned a master's degree in Human Performance and Recreation from the University of Southern Mississippi. In 2017, Macy became one of only 300 coaches in the country to receive a Certification in Emotional Intelligence (EQ). She has been inducted into the Hall of Fame at both Starmount High School and Greensboro College.

Connect with Heather at www.influenceandimpacters.com
On the website you can donate to the non-profit, purchase
apparel, videos, and books. In addition to FREE downloads
on the website you can also schedule clinics, camps, and
speaking events.

If you have additional questions reach us on
our *influence+impacters* HOTLINE at 252.493.6634 or
email Heather directly at
HeatherMacy@influenceandimpacters.com.

Stay connected with Influence and Impacters, Inc.

 2FTNinfluenceandimpacters
2FTNHeatherMacy

 @2FTNwithYou
@2FTNHeatherMacy

 Heather Macy

 Influenceandimpacters
Heather Macy

Made in the USA
Columbia, SC
17 February 2019